D0778394

INTRUSION DETECTION AND CORRELATION
Challenges and Solutions

Advances in Information Security

Sushil Jajodia
Consulting editor
Center for Secure Information Systems
George Mason University
Fairfax, VA 22030-4444
email: jajodia@gmu.edu

The goals of Kluwer International Series on ADVANCES IN INFORMATION SECURITY are, one, to establish the state of the art of, and set the course for future research in information security and, two, to serve as a central reference source for advanced and timely topics in information security research and development. The scope of this series includes all aspects of computer and network security and related areas such as fault tolerance and software assurance.

ADVANCES IN INFORMATION SECURITY aims to publish thorough and cohesive overviews of specific topics in information security, as well as works that are larger in scope or that contain more detailed background information than can be accommodated in shorter survey articles. The series also serves as a forum for topics that may not have reached a level of maturity to warrant a comprehensive textbook treatment.

Researchers as well as developers are encouraged to contact Professor Sushil Jajodia with ideas for books under this series.

Additional information about this series can be obtained from
http://www.wkap.nl/prod/s/ADIS

INTRUSION DETECTION AND CORRELATION
Challenges and Solutions

by

Christopher Kruegel
Fredrik Valeur
Giovanni Vigna

University of California, Santa Barbara, USA

 Springer

Library of Congress Cataloging-in-Publication Data

A C.I.P. Catalogue record for this book is available
from the Library of Congress.

INTRUSION DETECTION AND CORRELATION
Challenges and Solutions
by Christopher Kruegel, Fredrik Valeur and Giovanni Vigna
University of California, Santa Barbara, CA 93106 USA

Advances in Information Security Volume 14

ISBN 0-387-23398-9   e-ISBN 0-387-23399-7

Printed on acid-free paper.

Printed in the United States of America.

9 8 7 6 5 4 3 2 1   SPIN 11054276, 11332480

springeronline.com

Contents

List of Figures

List of Tables

Preface

The Internet is omnipresent and companies have increasingly put critical resources online. This has given rise to the activities of cyber criminals, and virtually all organizations face increasing threats to their networks and the services they provide. This book presents intrusion detection systems (IDSs) and addresses the problem of managing and correlating the alerts that are produced. We discuss the role of intrusion detection in the realm of network security and compare it to traditional methods such as firewalls and cryptography. We then analyze the challenges in interpreting and combining (i.e., correlating) alerts produced by these systems. Existing academic and commercial systems are classified and their advantages and shortcomings are presented, especially in the case of deployment in large, real-world sites.

Recently, IDSs have been increasingly pounded for failing to meet the expectations that researchers and IDS vendors were rising. Promises that IDSs are capable of reliably identifying malicious activity in large networks were premature and never turned into reality. While virus scanners and firewalls have visible benefits and remain virtually unnoticed during normal operations, the situation is different with intrusion detection sensors. State-of-the-art IDSs produce hundreds or even thousands of alerts every day. Unfortunately, almost all of these alerts are false positives, that is, they are not related to security-relevant incidents. Although tuning and proper configuration eliminate the most obvious false alerts, the problem of the vast imbalance between important and spurious notifications remains.

Researchers and IDS vendors have reacted and proposed alert correlation, an additional step intended to manage the alert flood and turn the raw sensor output into compact reports on the security status of the network under surveillance. The idea is to aggregate and group individual alerts into attack scenarios that provide a higher-level view of the activities on the network. Unfortunately, current systems fall short in dealing with the immense data volume that is produced by the sensors that are deployed in large network installations. In addition, dedicated nodes such as centralized processors become vulnerable to faults or targeted denial of service attempts and often represent performance bottlenecks. Another problem stems from the fact that it is often the case that sensor alerts are invalid. This causes the correlation process to deduce attack scenarios from incidents that have never occurred.

We address the aforementioned issues and present solutions that allow intrusion detection systems to be deployed in real-world installations to the benefit of the system administrator. Our proposed alert correlation process is realized by collaborating nodes that correlate and assemble the pieces of evidence, which are scattered over many hosts in the victim's network, into a single and coherent picture of ongoing attacks. The information of emerging threats is then fed back into the system and utilized to selectively adapt to data from suspicious sources. The main focus of our design is the protection of huge enterprise networks against coordinated attacks without being overwhelmed by the produced alert data and without failing because of the loss of a few critical correlation nodes. We also describe an approach to reduce the number of false positives by actively performing alert verification. The idea is to determine whether a potential attack has succeeded by checking for visible traces that this attack has left' on the system.

This book introduces solutions to practical problems that intrusion detection systems experience when deployed in large network installations. The reader is familiarized with the basics and concepts of this fast growing and fascinating field in network security and learns about state-of-the-art systems. We focus on current research problems and help the reader understand the limitations and advantages of intrusion detection systems and, in particular, alert correlation and mechanisms to detect false alarms.

Chapter 1

INTRODUCTION

> It is easy to run a secure computer system. You merely have to disconnect all dial-up connections and permit only direct-wired terminals, put the machine and its terminals in a shielded room, and post a guard at the door.
>
> — F.T. Gramp and R.H. Morris

As a matter of fact, computer systems are not operated this way. In order to provide useful services or to allow people to perform tasks more conveniently, computer systems are attached to networks. This resulted in the world-wide collection of local and wide-area networks known as the Internet. Although ease of use and convenience are tradeoffs with security, people often cannot or do not want to forfeit services provided by remote machines. Therefore, they have to deal with a loss of security.

When a computer system is attached to a network, three areas of increased risk can be identified [Cheswick and Bellovin, 1994]. First, the number of points that can potentially serve as the source of an attack against a computer is increased. For a stand-alone system, physical access to the machine is a prerequisite to an intrusion. When a system is connected to a network, each host that can send packets to the system can potentially be utilized by an intruder[1]. As certain services (such as web servers or name servers) need to be publicly available, each machine on the Internet might be the originator of malicious activity. This fact makes attacks very likely to happen on a regularly basis.

Second, the physical perimeter of the computer system is extended. For a single machine, everything is considered to be "inside a box" (or at least in close vicinity). The processor fetches data from memory which is read from secondary storage. Such data is (very well) protected from tampering

---

[1]The term intruder is used to describe persons with the malicious intent to gain unauthorized access to network resources.

and eavesdropping while transferred between the different components of the computers hardware. The same assumption is not true for data transferred over the network. Packets on the wire often pass areas and are forwarded by infrastructure devices that are completely out of the control of the receiver. Messages can be read, recorded, and later replayed, as well as modified on their journey. Especially in large networks such as the Internet, it is not trivial to authenticate the source that claims to be the message's origin.

Third, the number of services that networked machines typically offer is greater than the single authentication service offered by a stand-alone system. Although such a service (usually realized as login with password) may contain vulnerabilities, it is still only a single program which is comparatively simple. The authentication service mediates the ability to access files or to send e-mails through a single point. Networked computers, on the other hand, often offer by default a variety of remote connection possibilities to log in, access data, or relay mail. All service processes (called *daemons*) implementing remote access may contain exploitable program bugs or configuration errors that can lead to a security compromise.

The classical solutions to reduce the risks introduced by connecting computer systems to networks are firewalls and the use of cryptographic techniques.

Firewalls provide a parting line between the outside Internet (or untrusted third-party networks) and a trusted inside set of machines under the administrative control of the firewall owner. A firewall acts as a central point that allows one to regulate the accessibility of the services running behind it to hosts on the outside. This minimizes the number of potential targets and is similar to the situation where only a few controlled services (similar to the login service of a stand-alone system) can be publicly utilized.

The use of cryptographic techniques prevents the data from being read or modified when transferred over the network. The sender and the receiver agree upon a symmetric key or an asymmetric key pair that allows for the transformation of the sender's message (or cleartext) into the corresponding ciphertext and its reverse transformation back into the cleartext at the receiver's end. When properly applied, this cryptographic protection prevents attacks against data in transit. Notice, however, that the sender is not authenticated by simply encrypting the message. Additional mechanisms such as digital signatures and a trusted third party (called certification authority) are needed to provide strong authentication.

The strategies described above are important ways to improve the security of a computer system. Nevertheless, certain services (e.g. world wide web services and domain name services) are usually made available to everyone connected to the Internet. Therefore, they often cannot be strongly authenticated or blocked by firewalls.

1. Motivating Scenario

The following typical scenario describes the possible actions of an attacker and illustrates an additional security approach, which supports and augments the strategies sketched previously. We assume that the intruder is targeting a network installation run by a small company as depicted in Figure 1.1. In order to sell their products, the company has set up a small web site, called www.victim.com, which allows for online purchases. Being security aware, the web server is located behind a firewall which only allows inbound HTTP requests, secure HTTPS requests and DNS queries. The HTTP queries have to be permitted to transfer the web page requests and replies between users and the server. The secure HTTPS connection is used to cryptographically protect the customer's credit card information when it is transmitted to process the payments, and DNS queries have to be accepted to be able to resolve the victim.com domain names.

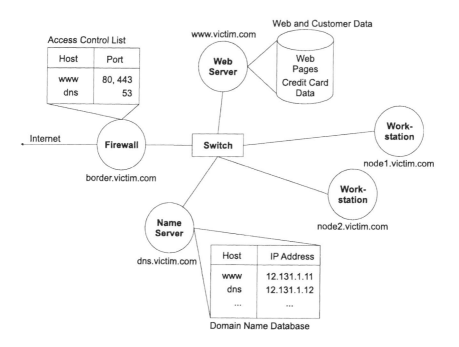

Figure 1.1. Victim Network Installation

A successful intrusion into a computer system is often divided into three stages [Asaka et al., 1999], which are called

- Surveillance (Reconnaissance) Stage,

- Exploitation Stage and

- Masquerading Stage.

During the surveillance stage, the attacker attempts to learn as much information as possible about its target and tries to discover vulnerable services as well as configuration errors. The exploitation stage includes elevating the attackers privileges by abusing an identified weakness. Finally, the masquerading stage covers all activity performed by an intruder after the successful break in (e.g., deleting log entries or patching the vulnerability used to get access).

In our example, the intruder starts the attack by obtaining the range of IP addresses owned or controlled by victim.com. This is done by querying the victim's DNS server. Next, a *portscan* is launched against each address that has been found in the previous step. Such a scan attempts to find running services on a machine by sending packets that pretend to establish a connection to interesting ports at the target host. When a server that is actually listening on a port being probed, it confirms the setup of the virtual connection with a reply packet. Otherwise an error message or no answer at all is returned. As the firewall in our example is properly configured, most of the connection request packets are discarded there. The attacker learns that only two machines provide a potential entry into the system, namely the DNS server and the web server.

The intruder chooses to attack the web server and attempts to learn the type and version of the server software. It is very common that a weakness in a service is tightly bound to a certain version of the program implementing it. In addition, it is important to know the underlying operating system and hardware architecture, because many exploits use short machine code programs (called *shellcode*) and rely on a specific memory layout. This layout and the architecture specific machine code obviously depend on both the operating system and the host architecture.

To obtain this information, the intruder retrieves the complete DNS entry for the web server from the domain name database. The web master is a diligent administrator and has filled in the hardware information field of the web server's DNS entry, identifying the server as running Windows 2000. This allows the attacker to conclude that the web server is a Microsoft Internet Information Service (IIS), an educated guess that can be verified by looking at the header of the reply to a standard web page request. For this product, a number of vulnerabilities have been discovered that allow an intruder to send a carefully crafted packet to exploit a buffer overflow weakness, thus obtaining administrator access.

The intruder downloads one of the exploit programs readily available on the Internet and gives it a try. As the administrator has not applied the latest patches, the attack is successful. The exploitation stage was very short. Notice that the firewall accepted and forwarded all relevant attack packets because everyone on the Internet is permitted to communicate with the company's web and name service. No violation against the access control policy has occurred. Nevertheless, an important network resource has been compromised. Also, encryption cannot be used to prevent this kind of attack. As the data is not modified by a third party during transmission, protecting the packet's payload is useless. Even the authentication of the sender would not be beneficial, as the origin of the attack is not disguised in our example. In addition, potential suspicious log entries at the server could later be removed by the attacker.

After the compromise, the intruder enters the masquerading stage and immediately starts to remove the marks of her attack by cleaning entries from the web server and the operating systems logs that relate to the host she used for the attack. In addition, she installs a *rootkit* - a collection of programs that replace system binaries with modified versions. The modified programs substitute administrative tools (e.g., file and process monitors) such that the actions of the attacker are hidden. In addition, rootkits often contain backdoor programs that provide an intruder means to log in to the compromised system at a later time.

Now, the attacker owns a new base for launching further attacks against other machines in the `victim.com` network. She can operate from a machine inside the network that is not subject to the firewall's access control. In addition, intrusions against other sites could be launched from the victim's hosts, hiding the true origin of the attacks.

The given example makes it obvious that firewalls and cryptography cannot defend computer systems against certain classes of malicious behavior. When a machine is connected to the Internet and has to provide publicly accessible services, it automatically becomes a target in a hostile environment. Although the installation of software updates and patches is beneficial and necessary, it is naive to assume that bug fixes will always be installed properly, before an attacker exploits the corresponding vulnerability.

This makes it necessary to install an additional defense to receive early warning about malicious activity and to cope with intrusions when the first perimeter of defense has been penetrated. Systems that attempt to detect malicious behavior that is targeted against a network and its resources are called *intrusion detection systems (IDSs)*. They are network security tools that process local audit data or monitor network traffic to identify evidence of an occurring attack. IDSs can either search for specific known patterns, called *signatures*, in their input stream (*misuse-based*) or detect certain deviations from expected behavior (*anomaly-based*) that indicate hostile activities against the protected network.

Intrusion detection systems constitute, besides firewalls and cryptography, the third building block of a secure computer system installation and can discover intrusions in all of the three stages of an intrusion. In our example, an IDS would have detected the huge amount of packets from a single source that are dropped at the firewall and indicate reconnaissance activity. Also, the IDS would have detected incoming packets containing malicious (exploit) payload and flag or drop suspicious messages. This would have potentially prevented the compromise of the web server in the example above. In addition, an IDS can also monitor the integrity of the host's files. When the attacker installs modified binaries, an IDS would have reported these modifications to the system administrator.

2.   Alert Correlation

While intrusion detection systems are efficient supplements to more traditional security mechanism, they are no panacea. An intruder may perform her surveillance over a long period of time or gather information directly from the DNS database, thus evading the detection capability of the intrusion detection system. Also, she can modify the exploit code obtained from the Internet to craft a packet that does not match existing signatures.

The problem is that although an attacker often leaves many traces at different spots in the target network during an intrusion attempt, most intrusion detection sensors consider these pieces independent of each other. Evidence of attacks against a network and its resources can be scattered over several hosts. Intrusion detection systems have to collect and relate alert information from different sources to spot complete attack scenarios such as the one described in the previous section. The process of collecting and relating alert information is called *alert correlation.*

Recently, alert correlation gained momentum and a number of academic and commercial correlation approaches have been suggested. However, there is no consensus on what this process is or how it should be implemented or evaluated. Many systems only implement a few aspects of the correlation process, such as the fusion of alerts that represent the detection of the same attack by different intrusion detection systems or the identification of multistep attacks that represent a sequence of actions performed by the same attacker.

One of the purposes of this book is to present alert correlation in its entirety, as an approach that is composed of a number of phases, each operating at different levels of abstraction and with different goals.

Furthermore, this book addresses fundamental challenges that are, in our opinion, not adequately addressed by current correlation systems. In particular the applicability of existing approaches is limited by two issues.

First, existing approaches operate under the assumption that the alert stream is composed of detections of successful attacks. Unfortunately, experience shows that this assumption is wrong. Intrusion detection systems are very noisy and, in addition to false positives, they produce alerts with different levels of relevance. As a consequence, the effectiveness of the correlation process is negatively affected by the poor quality of the input alert stream.

The book presents alert verification as a possible solution to this problem. The key idea of alert verification is to check whether an alert refers to a successful attack, given information about the configuration and setup of the network and the attached resources. When an attack is impossible with regard to this configuration, then the corresponding alert can be safely ignored.

Second, existing approaches realize the correlation process by forwarding alerts (i.e., evidence information) to a central node where the data is analyzed. As networks and traffic grow, this central nodes can become performance bottlenecks. Current approaches work reasonably well for mid-sized networks, but large installations with several thousand hosts push them to and above their limits. A scalable solution is necessary to allow for the correlation of events from different sources in the large enterprise networks. This requires a design where the total amount of traffic between all involved machines as well as the peak load at any single spot is manageable.

In this book, we present a completely distributed algorithm that can correlate alerts at different locations. Every node in the network acts as an equal partner in the detection process and collaborates with other nodes in a peer-to-peer fashion.

3. Organization

This book is organized as follows. Chapter 2 introduces the basic concepts of computer security and explains the key issues of the three main areas in network security, namely access control, cryptography, and intrusion detection. The generic architecture and features of intrusion detection systems are evaluated in more detail. Chapter 3 presents a general overview of alert correlation, while the following three chapters provide more details about individual stages of the alert correlation process. More precisely, Chapter 4 describes the challenges when collecting alerts from locations that are distributed over a network, and discusses issues in normalizing the information contained in alerts created by different sensors. Chapter 5 describes the early phases of the correlation process when analyzing alerts that are spatially and temporally related. Chapter 6 introduces phases that combine alerts into higher-level attack scenarios and evaluate their impact on the network and its services. Chapter 7 presents a distributed correlation framework that addresses scalability issues when performing alert correlation in very large network installations. Chapter 8 presents efforts to evaluate correlation systems and discusses the challenges of comparing different systems. Then, Chapter 9 discusses open issues in alert correlation. Finally, Chapter 10 briefly concludes.

Chapter 2

COMPUTER SECURITY
AND INTRUSION DETECTION

The scenario in the previous section described an exemplary threat to computer system security in the form of an intruder attacking a company's web server. This chapter attempts to give a more systematic view of system security requirements and potential means to satisfy them. We define properties of a secure computer system and provide a classification of potential threats to them. We also introduce the mechanisms to defend against attacks that attempt to violate desired properties.

Before one can evaluate attacks against a system and decide on appropriate mechanisms to fend off these threats, it is necessary to specify a *security policy* [Tanenbaum and van Steen, 2002]. A security policy defines the desired properties for each part of a secure computer system. It is a decision that has to take into account the value of the assets that should be protected, the expected threats and the cost of proper protection mechanisms. A security policy that is sufficient for the data of a normal home user may not be sufficient for a bank, as a bank is obviously a more likely target and has to protect more valuable resources.

1. Security Attacks and Security Properties

For the following discussion, we assume that the function of a computer system is to provide information. In general, there is a flow of data from a source (e.g., a host, a file, memory) to a destination (e.g., a remote host, another file, a user) over a communication channel (e.g., a wire, a data bus). The task of the security system is to restrict access to this information to only those parties (persons or processes) that are authorized to have access, according to the security policy in use.

The normal information flow and several categories of attacks that target it are shown in Figure 2.1 (according to [Stallings, 2000]).

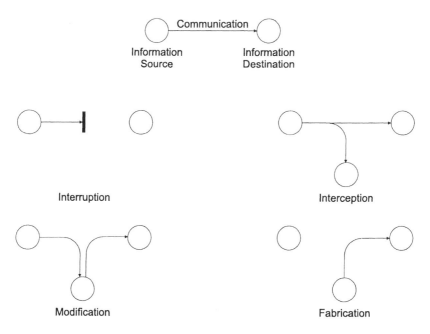

Figure 2.1. Security Attacks

1 **Interruption:** An asset of the system gets destroyed or becomes unavail-
able. This attack targets the source or the communication channel and prevents information from reaching its intended target (e.g., cutting the wire or
overloading the link so that the information gets dropped because of congestion). Attacks in this category attempt to perform a kind of *denial of
service (DOS)*.

2 **Interception:** An unauthorized party gets access to the information by
eavesdropping into the communication channel (e.g., by wiretapping).

3 **Modification:** The information is not only intercepted, but modified by an
unauthorized party while in transit from the source to the destination. (e.g.,
by modifying the message content).

4 **Fabrication:** An attacker inserts counterfeit objects into the system without
having the sender doing anything. When a previously intercepted object is
inserted, this processes is called *replaying*. When the attacker pretends to
be the legitimate source and inserts her desired information, the attack is
called *masquerading* (e.g., replaying an authentication message or adding
records to a file).

The four classes of attacks listed above violate different security properties
of the computer system. A security property describes a desired feature of a
system with regard to a certain type of attack. A common classification is listed
below [Coulouris et al., 1996; Northcutt, 1999].

- **Confidentiality:** This property covers the protection of transmitted data against its release to unauthorized parties. In addition to the protection of the content itself, the information flow should also be resistant against traffic analysis. Traffic analysis is used to gather other information than the transmitted values themselves from the data flow (e.g., the parties involved, timing data, or frequency of messages).

- **Integrity:** Integrity protects transmitted information against modifications. This property assures that a single message reaches the receiver as it has left the sender, but integrity also extends to a stream of messages. It means that no messages are lost, duplicated, or reordered and it makes sure that messages cannot be replayed. As destruction is also covered under this property, all data must arrive at the receiver. Integrity is not only important as a security property, but also as a property for network protocols. That is, message integrity must also be ensured in case of random faults, not only in case of malicious modifications.

- **Availability:** Availability characterizes a system whose resources are always ready to be used. Whenever information needs to be transmitted, the communication channel is available and the receiver can cope with the incoming data. This property makes sure that attacks cannot prevent resources from being used for their intended purpose.

- **Authentication:** Authentication is concerned with making sure that the information is authentic. A system implementing the authentication property assures the recipient that the data is from the source that it claims to be. The system must make sure that no third party can masquerade successfully as another source.

- **Non-repudiation:** This property describes the mechanism that prevents either sender or receiver from denying a transmitted message. When a message has been transferred, the sender can prove that it has been received. Similarly, the receiver can prove that the message has actually been sent.

2. Security Mechanisms

Different security mechanisms can be used to enforce the security properties defined in a given security policy. Depending on the anticipated attacks, different means have to be applied to satisfy the desired properties. Three main classes of measures against attacks can be identified, namely attack prevention, attack avoidance, and attack detection. They are explained in detail in the following sections.

2.1 Attack Prevention

Attack prevention is a class of security mechanisms that contains ways of preventing or defending against certain attacks before they can actually reach and affect the target. An important element in this category is access control, a mechanism which can be applied at different levels such as the operating system, the network, or the application layer.

Access control [Tanenbaum and van Steen, 2002] limits and regulates the access to critical resources. This is done by identifying or authenticating the party that requests a resource and checking its permissions against the rights specified for the demanded object. It is assumed that an attacker is not legitimately permitted to use the target object and is therefore denied access to the resource. As access is a prerequisite for an attack, any possible interference is prevented.

The most common form of access control used in multi-user computer systems are access control lists for resources that are based on the user and group identity of the process that attempts to use them. The identity of a user is determined by an initial authentication process that usually requires a name and a password. The login process retrieves the stored copy of the password corresponding to the user name and compares it with the presented one. When both match, the system grants the user the appropriate user and group credentials. When a resource should be accessed, the system looks up the user and group in the access control list and grants or denies access as appropriate. An example of this kind of access control can be found in the UNIX file system, which provides read, write and execute permissions based on the user and group membership. In this example, attacks against files that a user is not authorized to use are prevented by the access control part of the file system code in the operating system.

A firewall [Cheswick and Bellovin, 1994] is an important access control system at the network layer. The idea of a firewall is based on the separation of a trusted inside network of computers under single administrative control from a potential hostile outside network. The firewall is a central choke point that allows enforcement of access control for services that may run at the inside or outside. The firewall prevents attacks from the outside against the machines in the inside network by denying connection attempts from unauthorized parties located outside. In addition, a firewall may also be utilized to prevent users behind the firewall from using certain services that are outside (e.g., surfing web sites containing pornographic content).

2.2   Attack Avoidance

Security mechanisms in this category assume that an intruder may access the desired resource but the information is modified in a way that makes it unusable for the attacker. The information is preprocessed at the sender before it is transmitted over the communication channel and post-processed at the receiver. While the information is transported over the communication channel, it resists attacks by being nearly useless for an intruder. One notable exception are attacks against the availability of the information, as an attacker could still interrupt the message. During the processing step at the receiver, modifications or errors that might have previously occurred can be detected (usually because the information can not be correctly reconstructed). When no modification has taken place, the information at the receiver is identical to the one at the sender before the preprocessing step.

The most important member in this category is cryptography, which is defined as the science of keeping messages secure [Schneier, 1996]. It allows the sender to transform information into what may seem like a random data stream to an attacker, but can be easily decoded by an authorized receiver (see Figure 2.2).

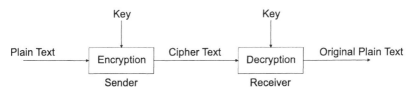

Figure 2.2. Encryption and Decryption

The original message is called *plaintext* (sometimes also cleartext). The process of converting this message through the application of some transformation rules into a format that hides its substance is called *encryption*. The corresponding disguised message is denoted as *ciphertext*, and the operation of turning it back into cleartext is called *decryption*. It is important to notice that the conversion from plain to ciphertext has to be lossless in order to be able to recover the original message at the receiver under all circumstances.

The transformation rules are described by a cryptographic algorithm. The function of this algorithm is based on two main principles: *substitution* and *transposition*. In the case of substitution, each element of the plaintext (e.g., bit, block) is mapped into another element of the used alphabet. Transposition describes the process where elements of the plaintext are rearranged. Most systems involve multiple steps (called rounds) of transposition and substitution to be more resistant against cryptanalysis. Cryptanalysis is the science of breaking the cipher, i.e., discovering the substance of the message behind its disguise.

When the transformation rules process the input elements in a continuous fashion, the mechanism is called a *stream cipher*. When the transformation operates on fixed sized input blocks, the corresponding encryption algorithm is called a *block cipher*.

If the security of an algorithm is based on keeping the way how the algorithm works (i.e., the transformation rules) secret, it is called a restricted algorithm. Those algorithms are no longer of any interest today because they do not allow standardization or public quality control. In addition, when a large group of users are involved, such an approach cannot be used. A single person leaving the group makes it necessary for everyone else to change the algorithm.

Modern crypto systems solve this problem by basing the ability of the receiver to recover encrypted information on the fact that she possesses a secret piece of information (usually called the *key*). Both encryption and decryption functions have to use a key and they are heavily dependent on it. When the security of the crypto system is completely based on the security of the key, the algorithm itself may be revealed. Although the security does not rely on the fact that the algorithm is unknown, the cryptographic function itself and the used key, together with its length, must be chosen with care. A common assumption is that the attacker has the fastest commercially available hardware at her disposal in her attempt to break the ciphertext.

The most common attack, called *known plaintext attack*, is executed by obtaining ciphertext together with its corresponding plaintext. The encryption algorithm must be so complex that even if the code breaker is equipped with plenty of such pairs, it is infeasible for her to retrieve the key. An attack is infeasible when the cost of breaking the cipher exceeds the value of the information, or the time it takes to break it exceeds the lifespan of the information itself.

Given pairs of corresponding cipher and plaintext, it is obvious that a simple key guessing algorithm will succeed after some time. The approach of successively trying different key values until the correct one is found is called *brute force* attack because no information about the algorithm is utilized. In order to be useful, it is a necessary condition for an encryption algorithm that brute force attacks are infeasible.

Depending on the keys that are used, one can distinguish two major cryptographic approaches - public-key and secret-key crypto systems.

Secret-Key Cryptography

Secret-key cryptography is the type of cryptography that has been used for the transmission of secret information for centuries, long before the advent of computers. These algorithms require that the sender and the receiver agree on a key before communication is started.

It is common for this variant (which is also called single-key or symmetric encryption) that a single secret key is shared between the sender and the receiver. It needs to be communicated in a secure way before the actual encrypted communication can start and has to remain secret as long as the information is to remain secret. Encryption is achieved by applying an agreed function to the plaintext using the secret key. Decryption is performed by applying the inverse function using the same key.

The classic example of a secret-key cipher which is widely deployed today is the *Data Encryption Standard (DES)* [DES, 1977]. DES has been developed in

1977 by IBM and adopted as a standard by the US government for administrative and business use. Recently, it has been replaced by the *Advanced Encryption Standard (AES - Rijndael)* [AES, 2001]. DES is a block cipher that operates on 64-bit plaintext blocks and utilizes a 56-bit key. The algorithm uses 16 rounds that are key dependent. Although there are no known weakness of the DES algorithm itself, its security has been much debated. The small key length makes brute force attacks possible and several cases have occurred where DES protected information has been cracked. A suggested improvement called 3DES uses three rounds of the simple DES with three different keys. This extends the key length to 168 bits while still relying on the very secure DES base algorithm.

Public-Key Cryptography

Before the advent of public-key cryptography, the knowledge of the key that is used to encrypt a plaintext also allowed the inverse process, the decryption of the ciphertext. In 1976, this paradigm of cryptography was changed by Diffie and Hellman [Diffie and Hellman, 1976] when they described their public-key approach. Public-key cryptography utilizes two different keys, one called the *public key*, the other one called the *private key*. The public key is used to encrypt a message while the corresponding private key is used to do the opposite. The innovation is the fact that it is infeasible to retrieve the private key given the public key. This makes it possible to remove the weakness of secure key transmission from the sender to the receiver. The receiver can simply generate her public/private key pair and announce the public key without fear. Anyone can obtain the public key and use it to encrypt messages that only the receiver, with the corresponding private key, is able to decrypt.

Mathematically, the process is based on the *trapdoor* of *one-way* functions. A one-way function is a function that is easy to compute but very hard to inverse. That means that given x it is easy to determine $f(x)$ but given $f(x)$ it is hard to get x. Hard is defined as computationally infeasible in the context of cryptographically strong one-way functions. Although it is obvious that some functions are easier to compute than their inverse (e.g., square of a value in contrast to its square root) there is no mathematical proof or definition of one-way functions. There are a number of problems that are considered difficult enough to act as one-way functions, but this is more an agreement among crypto analysts than a rigorously defined set (e.g., factorization of large numbers). A one-way function is not directly usable for cryptography, but it becomes so when a trapdoor exists. A trapdoor is a mechanism that allows one to easily calculate x from $f(x)$ when some additional information y is provided.

A common misunderstanding about public-key cryptography is thinking that it makes secret-key systems obsolete, either because it is more secure or because it does not have the problem of secretly exchanging keys. As the security of a crypto system depends on the length of the key used and the utilized transformation rules, there is no automatic advantage of one approach over the other. Although the key exchange problem is elegantly solved with a public-key system, the process itself is very slow and has its own problems. Secret-key systems are usually a factor of 1000 (see [Schneier, 1996] for exact numbers) faster than their public-key counterparts. Therefore, most communication is stilled secured using secret-key systems and public-key systems are only utilized for exchanging temporary secret keys which are then used to encrypt the communication. This hybrid approach is the common design, which benefits from the high speed of conventional cryptography and from the simplification of the key distribution process provided by public-key systems.

A problem in public-key systems is the authenticity of the public key. An attacker may offer the sender her own public key and pretend that it origins from the legitimate receiver. The sender then uses the fake public key to perform her encryption and the attacker can simply decrypt the message using her private key. This technique may be used to set up a man-in-the-middle attack in which a third party is able to monitor and modify the communication between two parties, even when encryption is used.

In order to thwart an attacker that attempts to substitute her public key for the victim's one, *certificates* are used. A certificate combines user information with the user's public key and the digital signature of a trusted third party that guarantees that the key belongs to the mentioned person. The trusted third party is usually called a *certification authority (CA)*. The certificate of a CA itself is usually verified by a higher level CA that confirms that the CA's certificate is genuine and contains its public key. The chain of third parties that verify their respective lower level CAs has to end at a certain point that is called the root CA. A user that wants to verify the authenticity of a public key and all involved CAs needs to obtain the self-signed certificate of the root CA via an external channel. Web browsers (e.g. Netscape Navigator, Internet Explorer), for example, ship with a number of certificates of globally known root CAs. A framework that implements the distribution of certificates is called a public key infrastructure (PKI). An important issue is revocation, the invalidation of a certificate when the key has been compromised.

The best known public-key algorithm and textbook classic is RSA [Rivest et al., 1978], named after its inventors Rivest, Shamir and Adleman. It is a block cipher in which the security of the messages is based on the infeasibility of the factorization of large integers, as the public and the private keys are functions of large primes. A well known protocol for public key management is X.509 [x509, 2002].

An interesting and important feature of public-key cryptography is its possible use for authentication. In addition to making the information unusable for attackers, a sender may utilize cryptography to prove her identity to the receiver. More precisely, by encrypting a message with her own private key a user can prove to another user that she is in fact the source of the message. The receiver can verify the identity of the sender by decrypting the message with the sender's public key. If the operation succeeds, the receiver can be confident that the message was sent by the sender. The process of encrypting a message with a users private key is called *signing* a message.

2.3   Attack Detection

Attack detection assumes that an attacker can obtain access to her desired targets and is successful in violating a given security policy. Mechanisms in this class are based on the optimistic assumption that, most of the time, the information is transferred without interference. When undesired actions occur, attack detection has the task of reporting that something went wrong and to react in an appropriate way. In addition, it is often desirable to identify the exact type of attack. An important facet of attack detection is recovery. Often it is enough to just report that malicious activity has been detected, but some systems require that the effects of an attack be reverted or that an ongoing and discovered attack is stopped. On one hand, attack detection has the advantage that it operates under the worst-case assumption that the attacker gains access to the communication channel and is able to use or modify the resource. On the other hand, detection is not effective in providing confidentiality of information. When the security policy specifies that interception of information has a serious security impact, then attack detection is not an applicable mechanism.

The most important members of the attack detection class are intrusion detection systems. Because this book is focused on intrusion detection and alert correlation, the remaining sections of this chapter are dedicated to a more detailed introduction to intrusion detection.

3.   Intrusion Detection

An intrusion is defined as a sequence of related actions performed by a malicious adversary that results in the compromise of a target system. It is assumed that the actions of the intruder violate a given security policy. The existence of a security policy that states which actions are considered malicious and should be prevented is a key requisite for an intrusion detection system. Violations can only be detected when actions can be compared against given rules.

Intrusion detection (ID) is the process of identifying and responding to malicious activities targeted at computing and network resources. This definition introduces the notion of intrusion detection as a process, which involves technology, people, and tools. Intrusion detection is an approach that is complementary with respect to mainstream approaches to security, such as access control and cryptography. The adoption of intrusion detection systems is motivated by several factors:

1 Surveys have shown that most computer systems are flawed by vulnerabilities, regardless of manufacturer or purpose [Landwehr et al., 1994], that the number of security incidents is continuously increasing [CERT, 2003], and that users and administrators are generally very slow in applying fixes to vulnerable systems [Rescorla, 2003]. As a consequence, many experts believe that computer systems will never be absolutely secure [Bellovin, 2001].

2 Deployed security mechanism, e.g., authentication and access control, may be disabled as a consequence of misconfiguration or malicious actions.

3 Users of the system may abuse their privileges and perform damaging activities.

4 Even if an attack is not successful, in most cases it is useful to be aware of the compromise attempt.

Intrusion detection systems (IDSs) are software applications dedicated to detect intrusions against a target network. IDSs have been designed to address the issues described above. As such, they are not intended to replace traditional security methods, but rather to complete them. According to [Dacier et al., 1999], an intrusion detection system has to fulfill the following requirements.

- *Accuracy* - An IDS must not identify a legitimate action in a system environment as an anomaly or a misuse (a legitimate action which is identified as an intrusion is called a *false positive*).

- *Performance* - The IDS performance must be sufficient enough to carry out real time intrusion detection (real time means that an intrusion has to be detected before significant damage has occurred – according to [Ranum, 2000] this should be under a minute).

- *Completeness* - An IDS should not fail to detect an intrusion (an undetected intrusion is called a *false negative*). One has to admit that it is rather difficult to fulfill this requirement because it is almost impossible to have a global knowledge about past, present, and future attacks.

- *Fault Tolerance* - An IDS must itself be resistant to attacks.

- *Scalability* - An IDS must be able to process the worst-case number of events without dropping information. This point is especially relevant for systems that correlate events from different sources at a small number of dedicated hosts. As networks grow bigger and get faster, such nodes become overwhelmed by the increasing number of events.

3.1   Architecture

There exist many IDSs, based on different conceptual frameworks. It is still possible, however, to recognize a common architecture that underlies all intrusion detection systems. We will present the main components of IDSs and their functionality.

To this end, we use the terminology introduced by the working group on the Common Intrusion Detection Framework (CIDF) [Porras et al., 1998]. CIDF models an IDS as an aggregate of four components with specific roles:

- *Event boxes (E-boxes).* The role of event boxes is to generate events by processing raw audit data produced by the computational environment.
  A common example of an E-boxes is a program that filters audit data generated by an operating system evaluated at the C2 level of TCSEC [U.S. Department of Defense, 1985]. Another example is a network sniffer that generates events based on the network traffic.

- *Analysis boxes (A-boxes).* The role of an analysis box is to analyze the events provided by other components. The results of the analysis are sent back to the system as additional events, typically representing alarms.
  Usually A-boxes analyze simple events supplied by E-boxes. Some A-boxes analyze events produced by other A-boxes and operate at a higher level of abstraction.

- *Database boxes (D-boxes).* Database boxes simply store events, guaranteeing persistence and allowing postmortem analysis.

- *Response boxes (R-boxes).* Response boxes consume messages that carry directives about actions to be performed as a reaction to a detected intrusion. Typical actions include killing processes, resetting network connections, and modifying firewall settings.

Figure 2.3 presents an IDS system where two E-boxes monitor the environment and deliver audit events to two A-boxes. These A-boxes analyze the audit data and provide their conclusions to a third A-box that correlates the alerts, stores them in a D-box and controls an R-box. Dashed lines are used to indicate exchange of events, solid lines represent the exchanging of raw audit data.

Note that components are logical entities which produce or consume events. The CIDF model does not mandate what their implementation should be. It only states their roles and interactions. They can be realized as a single process on a single computer or as a collection of cooperating processes spanning multiple computers.

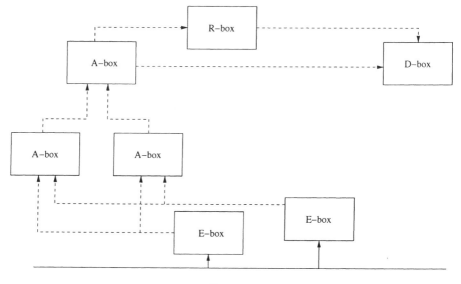

Figure 2.3. CIDF Description of an IDS System

3.2   Taxonomy

Intrusion detection systems may be classified according to different characteristics [Lunt, 1993; Allen et al., 2000; Bace and Mell, 2001]. The following ones seem to be particularly characterizing [Dacier et al., 1999]:

- *Detection method.* It defines the philosophy on which the A-box is built. Two approaches have been proposed. When the IDS defines what is "normal" in the environment and flags as attacks deviations from normality, it is qualified as *anomaly-based.* When the IDS explicitly defines what is "abnormal", using specific knowledge about the attacks in order to detect them, it is called *misuse-based.*

- *Behavior on detection.* It defines a characteristic of the R-box. It is said to be passive if the system just issues an alert when an attack is detected. If more proactive actions are taken (e.g., disconnecting users, shutting down network connections), it is said to be active.

- *Audit source location.* It specifies where the E-box takes audit data from. We distinguish between host-based IDSs, which deal with audit data generated on a single host, e.g., a C2 audit trail; application-based IDSs, which work on audit records produced by a specific application; and network-based IDSs, which monitor network traffic.

- *Usage frequency.* It discriminates between systems that analyze the data in real time and those that are run periodically (offline). It specifies how often the A-box analyzes data collected by other parts of the system.

We will analyze these characteristics more in detail in the following sections.

3.3 Detection Method

Detection can be performed according to two complementary strategies:

1 defining what is the manifestation of an attack and searching for an occurrence of the attack (misuse-based) or

2 defining what is the normal behavior on the system and searching for activities that deviate from it (anomaly-based).

Misuse-based Systems

Misuse-based systems are equipped with a database of information (the knowledge base) that contains a number of attack models (sometimes called "signatures"). The audit data collected by the IDS is compared with the content of the database and, if a match is found, an alert is generated. Events that do not match any of the attack models are considered part of legitimate activities.

The main advantage of misuse-based systems is that they usually produce very few false positives: attack description languages usually allow for modeling of attacks at such fine level of detail that only a few legitimate activities match an entry in the knowledge base.

However, this approach has drawbacks as well. First of all, populating the knowledge base is a difficult, resource intensive task. Furthermore, misuse-based systems cannot detect previously unknown attacks, or, at most, they can detect only new variations of previously modeled attacks. Therefore, it is essential to keep the knowledge base up-to-date when new vulnerabilities and attack techniques are discovered.

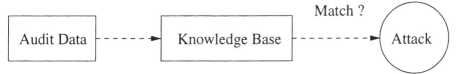

Figure 2.4. Block Diagram of a Typical Knowledge-Based IDS

A number of different techniques have been proposed for performing misuse-based intrusion detection [Ilgun et al., 1995; Lindqvist and Porras, 1999; Kumar and Spafford, 1994; Roesch, 1999; Neumann and Porras, 1999]. Before briefly discussing the most common misuse-based techniques, it is worth discussing how these systems can be differentiated on the basis of state maintenance (and the importance of this characteristic on the overall intrusion detection system).

A *stateless* intrusion detection system treats each event independently of others. When the processing of the current event is completed, every information regarding this event is discarded.

This approach simplifies the design of the system, specifically of the A-box, because it does not need to allocate and maintain memory to keep information about past activity. Stateless systems usually have very good performance in terms of speed of processing because the analysis step is reduced to simple lookups in the knowledge base and matches against the current event, with no additional operations needed.

However, stateless systems have important limitations. In the first place, they are not complete, in the sense that there exist classes of attacks that cannot be detected. For example, multistep attacks are malicious activities that require a series of steps to be completed. Actions involved in each step are not *per se* intrusive and become malicious only when executed in the correct and complete sequence. Because the system has no memory of past events, it lacks the possibility to keep track of steps. Note that it would be possible to model the entire attack on the basis of the last step, thus considering the action involved in this step as malicious, and inserting it in the attack knowledge base. However, because this action alone is not intrusive, it is likely to be performed also as part of legitimate activities. Thus, this approach would possibly generate an unacceptable number of false positives, thwarting the main advantage of misuse-based intrusion detection.

Furthermore, stateless systems are subject to a class of attacks whose aim is to trigger the generation of a flood of alerts. A number of tools have been proposed that analyze the database of attacks and automatically generate events or series of events that conform to the attack descriptions. The event stream synthesized in this manner forces intrusion detection systems to generate a large number of detection alerts. The resulting "alert storm" has been used to desensitize intrusion detection system administrators and hide attacks in the event stream [Patton et al., 2001; Mutz et al., 2003; Snot, 2004; Stick, 2004].

Stateful intrusion detection systems maintain information about past events. As a consequence, the effect of a certain event on the system is not independent of its position in the event stream. While this approach adds an additional level of complexity to the design and implementation of A-boxes, it provides significant advantages. In particular, stateful tools are able to model and detect attacks that involve many steps. Furthermore, they are less prone to the alert storm attacks described in the previous paragraph, because it is more difficult to develop a program that is able to exactly reproduce the steps of a modeled attack. However, these systems are all vulnerable to state-based attacks, where an attacker forces the IDS to maintain large amount of information about ongoing attacks, effectively affecting the overall performance of the system.

In signature-based systems, abstractions ("signatures") of attacks are stored in the knowledge base. Signatures are used to summarize in a compact format all the information necessary to describe attacks. For example, a network intrusion detection system may store in the knowledge base the content of network packets involved in known attacks. Usually, signatures are stored in a format that allows straightforward comparison with information found in the event stream. During operation, events are checked against entries in the signature file: if a match is found, the system raises an alarm.

Signature based systems have gained popularity because they are easy to develop, give accurate feedback on alarms, and are usually requires little computational resources.

However, they also have disadvantages:

- The description of an attack is usually a very low level description and thus, difficult to determine or interpret.

- Every attack or variation of an attack requires a new signature to be added to the knowledge base, thus its size can become very large.

- The more specific a signature is, the less false positives are generated. But also, the more specific a signature is, the easier it is for an attacker to create a slightly different version of an attack that do not match the signature and thus goes unnoticed. Such an attack is said to be *polymorphic.*

Example of signature-based systems include Snort [Roesch, 1999], EMERALD [Neumann and Porras, 1999] and many commercial products.

One technique that can be used to describe complex attack signatures are state transitions [Ilgun et al., 1995]. State transitions model an activity on the system as a series of state transitions, where a *state* is a snapshot of the system representing the value of all the memory locations of the system. Malicious activities move the state of the system from an initial safe state to a final compromised state, possibly passing through a number of intermediate states. This technique requires the analyst to identify those transitions that are critical in leading the system into a compromised state. The IDS will then search for such transitions. Of course, state transition systems are stateful tools.

State transition models are appealing because they allow high-level, even graphical, description of attacks. They have very high expressive power, meaning that arbitrarily complicated attacks can be modeled and detected. In particular, multistep attacks fit very well the state transition modeling technique. It also provides very detailed feedback on the generated alerts, because the entire sequence of actions that caused the alarm to be triggered can be easily provided. Furthermore, it allows to deploy a response before an attack reaches its final step, thus allowing to effectively prevent the attack rather than only detecting it.

The main disadvantage of the state transition technique is that its computational requirements can be high if the system has to keep track of many concurrent attacks.

Anomaly-based Systems

Anomaly-based systems are based on the assumption that all anomalous activities are malicious[1]. Thus, they first build a model of the normal behavior of the system (i.e., profile) and then look for anomalous activities, i.e., activities that do not conform to the established model. Anything that does not correspond to the system profile is flagged as intrusive [Helman and Liepins, 1993]. Many systems have been built following this approach, e.g., [Hofmeyr et al., 1998; Ghosh et al., 1998; Tan and Maxion, 2002; Ko et al., 1997].

Figure 2.5. Block Diagram of a Typical Behavior-Based IDS

The main advantage of systems based on this approach is that, in theory, they are able to detect previously unknown attacks. On the other hand, anomaly-based systems are prone to the generation of many false positives, that is, their accuracy is typically low.

One class of anomaly detection systems use machine learning techniques to determine the parameters of normal system behavior (i.e., system profiles). These systems may suffer from specific problems:

- The amount of time required to teach to the system the normal behavior might be long.

- The behavior of the monitored environment might change during a period of time, requiring the system to be retrained.

---

[1]Note that "All malicious activities are anomalous" is different from "All anomalous activities are malicious". The former implies that there do not exist malicious activities that are not anomalous and thus assumes that systems that detect every anomaly also detect every attack. On the other hand, the latter leaves open the possibility that there exist attacks that do not appear as anomalous activity. Thus, the "all malicious is anomalous" assumption postulates that anomaly-based systems can detect every possible attacks. The "all anomalous is malicious" asserts that attacks might go undetected by an anomaly-based IDS.

- If the training set contains attacks, the system will consider malicious behavior normal.

- It may be possible to perform an attack within the boundaries of "normality".

Statistical analysis has shown that, under reasonable assumptions, the probability $P(Intrusion|Alarm)$, i.e., the probability that an alarm really indicates an intrusion, is dominated by the false alarm rate rather than the true positive detection rate [Axelsson, 1999]. This is a consequence of the *base rate fallacy*: typical traffic shows a huge number of benign activities and only a few malicious events. The problem is that most systems today have poor performance in terms of suppression of false alarms.

A number of studies have indicated that most network systems are intrinsically characterized by a high rate of change and diversity [Floyd and Paxson, 2001]. Moreover, ambiguities in underlying protocols and differences in application programs exist [Bellovin, 1993]. Thus, detecting anomalous behavior in certain environments is very difficult, because anomalies are characteristic of the environment itself.

Finally, some new attack strategies have emerged that mimic legitimate activities and thus go undetected [Wagner and Soto, 2002; Tan et al., 2002]. While these studies were applied to a specific anomaly-based IDS, they are based on general concepts that seem to be applicable to whole classes of anomaly-based IDSs.

3.4 Type of Response

Most intrusion detection tools are passive: when an attack is detected, an alert is generated without trying to oppose the attack any further. This requires the security officer to manually inspect all alerts and take appropriate actions. Therefore, there can be a significant delay in the process of dealing with an intrusion.

A number of IDSs have proactive capabilities, e.g., they can change the security posture of a protected network to react to the detected attack. For example, such systems may modify file permissions, add firewall rules, kill processes, or shutdown network connections. It is important to note, however, that automatic countermeasures could, in certain cases, be leveraged by the attacker to damage the system itself or to cause a denial of service.

3.5 Audit Source Location

Intrusion Detection Systems can be characterized according to the source of the events they analyze. Typical system classes include host-based IDSs, application-based IDSs, network-based IDSs, as well as correlation systems. These are discussed in detail in the next paragraphs.

Host-based IDSs

Host-based IDSs (HIDS) detect attacks against a specific host by analyzing audit data produced by the host operating systems. Audit sources include:

- System information. Operating systems make available to processes in user space information about their internal working and security-relevant events. There exist programs that collect and show this information, e.g., *ps, vmstat, top, netstat.* The information provided is usually very complete and reliable because it is retrieved directly from the kernel. Unfortunately, few operating systems provide mechanism to systematically and continuously collect this information.

- Syslog facility [Lonvick, 2001]. Syslog is an audit facility provided by many UNIX-like operating systems. It allows programmers to specify a text message describing an event to be logged. Additional information, like the time when the event happened and the host where the program is running, is automatically added. Because of their simplicity, syslog events are used extensively by applications. However, applications usually log information valuable for debugging purposes that is not necessarily tailored to the needs of intrusion detection. Furthermore, a specific audit format is not imposed by the facility but changes according to the program that uses it. Thus, it may be difficult to extract audit data from logs and perform sophisticated analysis. Finally, the logged information can be easily polluted by messages crafted by an attacker to cover her tracks.

- C2 audit trail. Some operating systems comply with the C2 level of the TCSEC standard and thus monitor the execution of system calls. The data obtained is accurate because it comes directly from within the kernel.

Application-based IDS

Application-based IDSs detect attacks against a specific application. The audit information necessary to perform intrusion detection is usually obtained either using the already described syslog facility or instrumenting the application with specific audit mechanisms. The following discussion will focus on the latter approach.

Adding audit mechanisms to an existing application requires the modification of the application so that it produces audit information in response to security-relevant events. This can be accomplished in different ways:

- Directly modifying the application source code to include auditing code. This approach requires that the application code be available and modifiable.

- Interposing code responsible to extract audit information in correspondence of interfaces used by the application, e.g., the system call or the standard C library interface. One disadvantage of this approach is that applications other than the one to be monitored could be affected, e.g., in terms of performance loss, by the use of the interposition mechanism.

- Using extension hooks provided by the application itself to implement the audit collection functionality. This approach guarantees great flexibility, but not all the applications offer extension hooks.

A description of a tool performing intrusion detection at the application level can be found in [Almgren and Lindqvist, 2001]. This system leverages the extension mechanism of the Apache web server to implement an audit data source. The collected audit information is used to monitor the behavior of the web server.

Network-based IDSs

Network-based IDSs (NIDSs) detect attacks by analyzing the network traffic exchanged on a network link. Therefore, in network-based IDSs, the E-boxes are network sniffers.

The analysis of the content of network packets can be performed at different levels of sophistication, e.g., performing simple pattern matching on the header and/or the payload of a packet, or exploiting knowledge about the protocol followed by the communication. Higher-level analysis supports more sophisticated analysis of the data, but it is usually slower and requires more resources.

Network-based IDSs are very appealing because they are easy to deploy, and have a minimal or no impact on the monitored hosts. On the other hands, changes in network technology could impair the usefulness of NIDSs:

- High-speed networks might increase the network throughput beyond the capabilities of sniffers.

- Switched networks make it more difficult to choose the location where the NIDSs should be placed.

- The adoption of encryption of the communications reduces or completely prevents NIDSs from accessing the contents of network connections.

Furthermore, studies have shown that, if particular care is not taken, NIDSs are vulnerable to a class of attacks (called insertion and evasion) that take advantage of the physical and logical separation of the NIDSs from their monitored hosts to undermine their detection capability. [Ptacek and Newsham, 1998; Malan et al., 2000; Handley et al., 2001].

3.6   Usage Frequency

Dynamic intrusion detection tools analyze in real time the activity of the system to be protected. Audit data is examined as soon as it is produced. The advantage of this approach is that system activities can be analyzed timely and thus, a proper response can be issued when an attack is detected. However, real-time collection and analysis of audit data may introduce a significant overhead.

Static tools are run offline at specific intervals. They analyze a snapshot of the system state and produce an evaluation of the security of that state. They do not provide any security in between two consecutive runs, and therefore, in case of a successful attack, they can be used only for postmortem analysis. However, by running only occasionally, they may perform a more thorough analysis without having an unacceptable impact on the performance of the monitored system.

3.7   IDS Cooperation and Alert Correlation

A recent trend in intrusion detection is to use, at the same time, different intrusion detection systems and correlate the analysis results and corresponding alerts. This approach aims at achieving higher-level descriptions of attacks or a more condensed view of the security issues highlighted during the analysis.

A number of requirements and possible application scenarios for IDS interoperation have been described [Kahn et al., 1998]. For example, two IDSs might cooperate in the following ways:

- Analyzing each other's generated alerts. This would be especially useful if they use different detection techniques, e.g., one IDS is anomaly-based and the other one is misuse-based.

- Complementing each other's coverage, e.g., two IDSs may be both host-based but located on two different hosts involved in an attack. These IDSs would produce an aggregate report on the malicious activity.

- Reinforcing each other's alerts to keep the number of false positives low.

Alert correlation is a multistep process that receives alerts from different intrusion detection systems as input and produces a high-level description of the malicious activity on the network. The core of this book describes the different phases of the correlation process and the challenges associated with each phase. We emphasize open problems and discuss current approaches to solve some of the issues. After a detailed discussion of the correlation phases, we present an approach to perform distributed correlation in Chapter 7 that addresses scalability requirements for correlation in very large network installations.

Chapter 3

ALERT CORRELATION

Alert correlation is a process that takes as input the alerts produced by one or more intrusion detection sensors and provides a more succinct and high-level view of occurring or attempted intrusions. The main objective is to produce intrusion reports that capture a high-level view of the activity on the network without losing security-relevant information.

The notion of security-relevant information cannot be completely objective as it depends on a site's *security policy*. A security policy defines the desired properties for each part of a secure site's installation. It is a decision that has to take into account the value of the assets that should be protected, the expected threats and the cost of proper protection mechanisms. A security policy that is sufficient for the data of a normal user at home may not be sufficient for bank applications, as these systems are obviously a more likely target and have to protect more valuable resources. Therefore, it is important that a correlation scheme can be adjusted to accommodate different requirements of different security policies.

The alert correlation process consists of a collection of components that transform sensor alerts into intrusion reports. Because alerts can refer to different kinds of attacks at different levels of granularity, the correlation process cannot treat all alerts equally. Instead, it is necessary to provide a set of components that focus on different aspects of the overall correlation task.

Some of the components can operate on all alerts, independent of their type. These components are used in the initial and final phase of the correlation process to implement general functionality that is applicable to all alerts. Other components can only work with certain classes of alerts. These components are responsible for performing specific correlation tasks that cannot be generalized for arbitrary alerts.

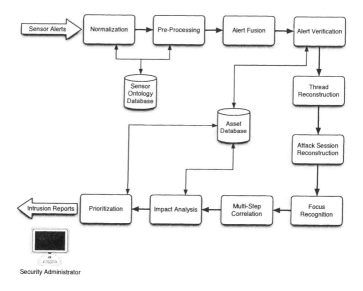

Figure 3.1. Correlation Process Overview

Figure 3.1 gives a graphical representation of the alert correlation process. The core of this process consists of components that implement specific functions, which operate on different spatial and temporal properties. That is, some of the components correlate events that occur close in time and space (e.g., alerts generated on one host within a small time window), while others operate on events that represent an attack scenario that evolves over several hours and that includes alerts that are generated on different hosts (e.g., alerts that represent large-scale scanning activity). It is natural to combine events that are closely related (spatially and temporally) into composite alerts, which are in turn used to create higher-level alerts.

In the process shown in Figure 3.1, alerts that are correlated by one component are used as input by the next component. However, it is not necessary that all alerts pass through the same components sequentially. Some components can operate in parallel, and it is even possible that alerts output by a sequence of components are fed back as input to a previous component of the process. That is, even though the process is represented as a "pipeline" for the sake of presentation, some components of the process may be applied multiple times, may be applied in parallel, or may be applied in a different order.

The correlation process should be carried out without losing relevant information (given a site's security policy). To this end, there are two types of operations that can always be performed without losing relevant information. The first type of operations combine a number of alerts into a single meta-alert that represents all individual members. Two examples are a set of probe packets that are summarized as a portscan and the merging of multiple steps of an attack into a higher-level alert that represents these steps. The second type of operation includes those that identify and discard (or appropriately tag) false or irrelevant alarms. The assumption is that when a sensor incorrectly identifies an event as an attack the alert should be excluded from the correlation process. Both types of operations are applied throughout the correlation process and several concrete examples are discussed later in this book when the different correlation components are described in more detail.

For the discussion in this book, we assume that the alert correlation process receives as input a stream of alerts $\{A_1, A_2, \ldots, A_i, \ldots\}$ from different intrusion detection sensors that are defined as follows:

Definition:

> An alert A is a list of n pairs of attributes a_i with their corresponding value sets v_i, that is, $A = \{(a_1, v_1), (a_2, v_2), \ldots, (a_n, v_n)\}$. Each attribute a_i of an alert describes a certain property (or feature) of the attack that this alert refers to (e.g., name and target of the attack).

An attribute has a type (e.g., string, or IP address) and a set of values v associated with it. The value set v can be empty when the attribute does not apply to the attack (e.g., in case of attributes specifying network-level properties for a host-based attack) or when no information has been supplied by the sensor that generated the alert.

When two or more related alerts are merged as part of the alert correlation process, the result is called a *meta-alert*. A meta-alert is similar to an alert but its contents (e.g., the victims of an attack) are derived as a function of the attributes of the merged alerts. Each meta-alert also contains references to all of the alerts that were merged to produce the meta-alert. The decision of whether alerts should be merged or not is dependent on the particular component of the correlation process and on the values of relevant attributes of these alerts.

A meta-alert can be further merged with other alerts (either sensor alerts or meta-alerts), resulting in a hierarchical structure, which can be represented as a tree. The most recent meta-alert is the root node in this tree, and all successor nodes can be reached by following the references to the merged alerts. All intermediate nodes in the tree are meta-alerts, while all leaves are sensor alerts. The purpose of meta-alerts is to aggregate information of related attacks and present a single alert instance that summarizes all the relevant information to a human analyst.

Whenever the correlation system considers a meta-alert and a sensor alert as candidates for merging, it first attempts to merge the root of the meta-alert with the sensor alert. If the root alert cannot be merged, all its successor alerts are *independently* considered for merging. The process of finding appropriate alert candidates for merging is repeated recursively until an alert that can be merged with the sensor alert is found, or until a leaf alert is reached. The idea behind this approach is the fact that a meta-alert represents the complete attack information of all its successor nodes. Therefore, alerts are considered in a top-down fashion and merging is performed at the highest level possible.

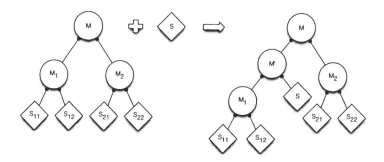

Figure 3.2. Alert Merging Process

Consider the following example of merging a meta-alert M, which has two successor nodes M_1 and M_2, and a sensor alert S, as shown in Figure 3.2. The correlation system first checks whether M and S can be merged, but fails. Next, M_1 is considered for merging with S. This operation is successful, and a new meta-alert M' with two children (M_1 and S) is created. The correlation process continues to consider M_2 and S for merging, because successor nodes are considered independently. Note, however, that no children of M_1 will be considered, because a successful merge with a node precludes all of this node's successors from being candidates.

To explain the different components of the correlation process, the following attack scenario example is used throughout the next chapters of this book. In this example, a victim network is running a vulnerable Apache web service on a Linux host (IP: 10.0.0.1). This host runs a host-based IDS (H) and an application-based IDS (A) that monitors the web logs for entries that indicate malicious activity. In addition, the network traffic is analyzed by two different network-based IDSs (N1 and N2). Table 3.1 shows the seven alerts (Alert 1 through Alert 7) that are generated during an attack against the victim host. The attack is as follows.

The attacker (IP: 31.3.3.7) first launches a portscan against the Linux host and discovers the vulnerable Apache server (Alert 2, Alert 3). While the scan is in progress, a worm (IP: 80.0.0.1) attempts to exploit a Microsoft IIS related vulnerability and fails (Alert 1). After the scan finished, the attacker launches a successful Apache buffer overflow exploit (Alert 4, Alert 5) and obtains an interactive shell, running as the Apache user. Using a local exploit against linuxconf (a system administration tool), the attacker elevates her privileges

ID	Name	Sensor	Start/End	Source	Target	Tag
1	IIS Exploit	N1	12.0 / 12.0	80.0.0.1	10.0.0.1, port:80	
2	Scanning	N2	10.1 / 14.8	31.3.3.7	10.0.0.1	
3	Portscan	N1	10.0 / 15.0	31.3.3.7	10.0.0.1	
4	Apache Exploit	N1	22.0 / 22.0	31.3.3.7	10.0.0.1, port:80	
5	Bad Request	A	22.1 / 22.1		localhost, Apache	
6	Local Exploit	H	24.6 / 24.6		linuxconf	
7	Local Exploit	H	24.7 / 24.7		linuxconf	

Table 3.1. Attack Scenario Alerts

and becomes `root`. Note that the same exploit is executed twice with different parameters (Alert 6, Alert 7) before it succeeds.

Given this attack scenario, the correlation system should present the administrator with a single meta-alert that characterizes a multistep attack against the victim host. The multistep attack consists of three steps: the initial scanning, the remote attack against the web server, and the privilege escalation. The two alerts (Alert 2, Alert 3) describing the scanning incident should be merged and marked as referring to a single incident. The two alerts referring to the web server attack (Alert 4, Alert 5) should be merged as being part of the same remote exploit. The two alerts associated with the privilege escalation (Alert 6, Alert 7) should be merged because they represent repeated instances of the same local attack. The alert raised because of the worm activity should be excluded from the scenario and marked as irrelevant.

In Table 3.1, the *ID* and *Name* columns identify a certain alert, the *Start/End* column shows the start time and end time of the corresponding attack and the *Source* and *Target* columns list all information about the attack's sources and targets. The column *Tag* is included to show information that the correlation system associates with each alert (e.g., references to successor nodes for meta-alerts or indications of irrelevant alerts).

In the following chapters, the components of the correlation process and their goals are explained in detail. Using the example scenario introduced above, we will show the operations that the correlation phases perform on the individual alerts.

Chapter 4

ALERT COLLECTION

The task of the alert correlation process is to combine alerts from different sources to obtain a better overview of the activity on the network. This implies that the alerts provided as input to the correlation process should be collected from a variety of different intrusion detection sensors. Possibly, these sensors operate on data from different domains and analyze both host-based and network-based events. Because of the variety of events that are analyzed, alerts from different sensors contain different domain-specific pieces of information. In addition, because sensors are implemented by different vendors or research groups, the same piece of information might also be denoted using different names and formats.

The alert correlation process, by its nature, has to deal with very diverse input alerts that differ in content and in the way this content is represented. Therefore, it is necessary to transform raw input alerts into a standardized format that is suitable for further processing. It is the task of the initial phases of the correlation pipeline to collect data from different sources and process them so that later phases can operate on well-defined objects. As part of this transformation, it is often necessary to supply values for the attributes that are needed by many correlation steps (such as name, start time, end time, source, and destination).

Two major issues in any distributed system are time and synchronization. In the case of alert correlation, the process receives input alerts from multiple sensors that are often placed at different, distributed locations in the network. Two important attributes of these input alerts are timestamps, which are used to establish causal relationships between alerts. In order to identify the correct causal relationships, it is necessary that the timestamps are accurate and reflect the actual order of occurrence. When an event at sensor X happens before an event at sensor Y, it is necessary that the timestamps of the corresponding alert messages, which are sent to the correlation system, reflect this order. Much research has been done on the problems of physical and logical clocks and timestamps in distributed systems. It is part of the alert collection phases to ensure that timestamp attributes receive meaningful values before passing the alerts to later stages of the pipeline.

This chapter presents the challenges that correlation systems face when collecting alerts from different intrusion detection sensors. The problems of a standardized syntax and semantics for alerts are discussed, as well as the problem of supplying necessary attribute values, especially the inclusion correct timestamps in a distributed setup.

1.　Alert Normalization

Alert messages are produced by a variety of sensors developed by different vendors and research groups. Because these alert messages can be encoded in different formats, it is necessary to translate each alert into a standardized format that is understood by the alert correlation process. This translation, or *normalization*, implies that the syntax and semantics of a sensor alert is recognized.

The intrusion detection community early recognized the problem of interoperability and the Common Intrusion Detection Framework (CIDF) was created. The CIDF was an effort to develop protocols and application programming interfaces so that intrusion detection research projects could share information and resources, and, in addition, so that intrusion detection components could be reused. Some of the concepts and ideas proposed as part of the CIDF effort encouraged the creation of an Internet Engineering Task Force (IETF) working group, named the Intrusion Detection Working Group (IDWG).

The purpose of the Intrusion Detection Working Group is to define data formats and exchange procedures for sharing information of interest to intrusion detection and response systems, and to management systems which may need to interact with them. The main outcome was the Intrusion Detection Message Exchange Format [Curry and Debar, 2003] data model (IDMEF). IDMEF provides a standard representation for intrusion alerts. This representation defines the syntax of an alert and specifies the semantics of certain attributes. However, the IDMEF effort is mostly concerned with syntactic rules. It is possible, and common, that sensor implementors choose different names for the same attack[1], provide incomplete information for certain fields, or choose to include additional fields to store relevant data. As a result, similar information can be labeled differently or can be included in different fields. Because there is no

---

[1]There is no mandatory naming convention, and currently a few different competing schemes such CVE [CVE, 2004] or Bugtraq IDs [Bugtraq, 2004] exist.

specification for the content of most fields, they can be filled with meaningless strings (most commonly, "unknown" is used).

We believe that the intrusion detection community would benefit greatly from a shared alert model that extends the current IDMEF work with semantic information and a common attack naming scheme. An ontology for intrusions is a prerequisite for true interoperability between different IDSs. A recent paper [Undercoffer et al., 2003] presented an initial intrusion detection ontology. However, refinement is still necessary to capture low-level attributes at both the network and the operating system level. Without a common way of describing all involved entities, sensors will continue to send reports that appear to disagree even when detecting the same intrusion.

In current alert correlation systems, adapter modules are used to interface with different intrusion detection sensors. Each module relies on a knowledge base to convert sensor-specific information into attributes and values usable by the correlator. In order to facilitate convergence, a newly designed alert correlation system should take alert names from the CVE (Common Vulnerabilities and Exposures) [CVE, 2004] list, which is a well-known effort to standardize the names for all publicly known vulnerabilities.

Given the alerts of the example scenario as outlined in Chapter 3, the alert normalization phase would assign identical names to the two alerts describing the portscan (Alert 2, Alert 3) as shown in Table 4.1. All other alerts receive appropriate CVE identifiers depending on the attacks they refer to. Throughout this paper, however, we will continue to use the original names for the sake of readability. Changes in the table are shown in bold face.

ID	Name	Sensor	Start/End	Source	Target	Tag
1	IIS Exploit	N1	12.0 / 12.0	80.0.0.1	10.0.0.1, port:80	
2	**Portscan**	N2	10.1 / 14.8	31.3.3.7	10.0.0.1	
3	Portscan	N1	10.0 / 15.0	31.3.3.7	10.0.0.1	
4	Apache Exploit	N1	22.0 / 22.0	31.3.3.7	10.0.0.1, port:80	
5	Bad Request	A	22.1 / 22.1		localhost, Apache	
6	Local Exploit	H	24.6 / 24.6		linuxconf	
7	Local Exploit	H	24.7 / 24.7		linuxconf	

Table 4.1. Alert Normalization

2. Alert Preprocessing

Normalized alerts are denoted by a standardized name and have attributes that are in a format that is understood by the correlation system. However, an additional preprocessing phase is required because certain sensors omit some of the fields that are important for the correlation process (i.e., start time, end time, source, and target).

2.1   Determining the Alert Time

First, the start time and the end time have to be determined for each alert. The start time of an event is defined as the point in time when this event occurs. The end time of an event is defined as the point in time when an event ends. The difference between the end time and the start time denotes the duration of the event. Depending on the event's class, the start time and end time do not necessarily have to be different. An example for an event without a duration is the detection of a single network packet. In this case, the start and end times are both set to the point in time when the packet is received by the sensor. An example for an event with a duration is a portscan that consists of multiple packets. Here, the start time denotes the first packet of the scan while the end time denotes the last packet.

The IDMEF standard defines the following three different classes to represent time.

1 `CreateTime`: This is the time when the alert is created by the analyzer. This is the only timestamp considered mandatory by the IDMEF standard.

2 `DetectTime`: This is the time when the event(s) producing an alert are detected by the analyzer. In the case of more than one event, the time the first event was detected.

3 `AnalyzerTime`: This is the time at the analyzer when the alert is sent to a correlation system (which is called manager in the IDMEF terminology).

All three timestamps can be provided by intrusion detection sensors before sending alerts to the alert correlator. Considering these three types of timestamps, the `DetectTime` is the first candidate to be used as the start time attribute. However, the alert correlation process relies extensively on timestamps to deduce relationships between events, and thus it is important that the time values are accurate. Directly using the timestamps supplied in the alert messages might lead to incorrect results. It is possible for a sensor X to assign a later `DetectTime` to an event A than a sensor Y to another event B, although event A happens before event B. This could simply happen because the clocks of sensor X and sensor Y are not synchronized and the clock of sensor X is later than the clock of sensor Y.

The IDMEF standard acknowledges this problem, but considers it as outside of the scope of the specification. The following paragraphs discuss different approaches to assign accurate start and end times to events.

A straightforward solution is to discard the timestamps in the alert message altogether and use the time at the correlator when a message is received as the alert's start time. This solution sacrifices correctness for ease of implementation, because it is possible that a later message sent from sensor Y arrives at the correlation system before another message that was sent earlier from sensor X. This is possible when the interval between two events detected by two different sensors is in the same order of magnitude as the time it takes to send a message from a sensor to the correlator.

A slight improvement can be realized when the AnalyzerTime is available in the alert message. As mentioned above, whenever a sensor sends an IDMEF message to the correlator, it should place the current value of its real-time clock in the AnalyzerTime field. This should occur as late as possible in the message transmission process, ideally right before the message is "put on the wire" When a correlator then receives an IDMEF message, it should compute the difference between its own real-time clock and the time in the AnalyzerTime element of the message. This difference can then be used to adjust the values of the other timestamps and the adjusted DetectTime or CreateTime can be used as start time.

In both cases, the correlation process should not strictly enforce an order on two alerts that are received within a short period of time. That is, when alert message A is received by the correlator a short time before alert message B, the correlation process should consider both possible relationships (i.e., $A \rightarrow B$ and $B \rightarrow A$) as valid. The exact definition of "a short period of time" depends on the setup of the sensors and the correlator. When messages can be expected to travel fast between different entities (e.g., in a local area network), the period can be in the range of milliseconds. When messages are sent over larger distances or use public Internet links, the period could be as long as a few seconds.

A better solution uses clocks that are synchronized to an external source such as NTP or SNTP, GPS/GOES/WWV clocks, or some other reliable time standard. In this case, the timestamps that are assigned by the intrusion detection sensors can be directly used by the correlation system. When using the timestamps that are contained in an IDMEF alert message, the correlator uses, in this order, the DetectTime, the CreateTime, or the AnalyzerTime to assign a value to the event's start time.

Even with synchronized physical clocks, lost alert messages could present a problem for the correlation process. Consider the following situation: sensor X and sensor Y both send alerts at time t, and both these messages arrive at the correlator. Then, sensor X transmits a message at time $t + 1$ which is lost due to congestion. Later, at time $t + 2$, sensor Y transmits an alert that is immediately received by the correlation system. Eventually, the loss of the alert sent by sensor X is detected (e.g., because of a missing acknowledgment) and the message is sent again at time $t + 3$. If the correlation system has already processed the previous three messages received at times t and $t + 2$ and also cannot deal with out-of-order alerts, the message sent by sensor X at $t + 1$ cannot be considered.

To defeat this problem, all alert messages could be buffered for a certain amount of time before being forwarded to the next phases of the correlation process. Again, a time period needs to be specified that depends on the setup of the system and the probability of dropping messages. A better solution is based on a periodic synchronization approach. The idea is that all sensors and the correlator agree to send synchronization records at certain intervals. For each interval, the correlator must make sure that all clients have sent synchronization records before proceeding to process the alerts received in this interval.

An interesting alternative solution that does not require synchronized physical clocks is based on logical timestamps. This solution can be used when timestamp attributes are only utilized to recognize potential relationships between alerts that are reported from distributed intrusion detection sensors.

Logical timestamps can be used when the following three assumptions hold:

1 **Each host that is part of the protected network installation is equipped with a sensor.** Logical timestamps implement a distributed collaboration algorithm. For these schemes to work, it is required that all nodes are participating and correctly following the protocol. In the context of alert correlation, it is required that all hosts on the network run sensors that are aware of the logical timestamp protocol.

2 **No out-of-band relationships between events that occur at different hosts.** When two different events A and B are detected by two different sensors X and Y, A and B can only be related if a message is sent from the host where sensor X is located to the host where sensor Y is located. This message has to be sent *after* event A has occurred at X and it has to be received by Y *before* B has occurred. That is, an event at a host is only related to an event at another host if there is information transmitted between these hosts that is observable by the sensors.

   An example for a out-of-band relationship between two remote events is a human that writes down the output of a program at one location, walks over to another host, and uses the data as input for a program there. In this case, the flow of information between two hosts is not observable by sensors that are located on the two hosts.

3 **The sending and receiving of messages between hosts is observable by the sensors.** This is necessary to correctly update the sensors' local clocks.

Logical timestamps are particularly useful when dealing with host-based intrusion detection sensors that are distributed over a network. In this case, each sensor's view is restricted to events that occur locally at the host where the sensor is installed. Messages are represented by network packets that are sent between hosts. Whenever an event occurs at a host X, it is reasonable to assume that a second event at a remote host Y can only be caused by the first event when some network packets have been transmitted from X to Y.

Logical clocks as a mechanism for synchronizing events in distributed systems have been introduced by Lamport [Lamport, 1978]. Each sensor has a logical clock, which is a strict monotonically increasing software counter whose value need not have any particular relationship to any existing physical clock. Each sensor C keeps its own logical clock C_s, which is used by a sensor to assign timestamps to alert messages when they are sent to the correlator as well as to tag messages that are sent between the hosts where the sensors are located.

To capture a potential relationship between events, sensors update their logical clocks as well as piggyback the values of their logical clocks on messages that are sent to other hosts according to the following three rules.

1 C_s is incremented whenever the sensor observes a local input event **and** before a message is sent.

2 When a host sends a message m, the colocated sensor piggybacks on m the value $t = C_s$ of its current logical clock.

3 When a host receives a message m with timestamp t, the colocated sensor s' sets its logical clock to $C_{s'} = \max(C_{s'}, t)$.

While it is relatively easy to develop a sensor that implements the first and the third rule, it is not trivial to implement the second rule. This second rule essentially states that outgoing messages (i.e., network packets) have to be intercepted before the are "put on the wire" and extended with the value of the local timestamp.

We have designed a solution to efficiently exchange timestamp information in a message based distributed system that is based on piggybacking information onto IP packets. The primary design goal was to minimize the introduced overhead. As network traffic between nodes can be very high, only a lightweight solution is acceptable. To achieve this goal, no additional information is added to regular packets, only the "IP identification" field in the IP header is modified (in compliance with RFC 791 [Postel, 1981]). The scheme has been implemented as a kernel module for Linux. The interested reader is referred to [Kruegel and Toth, 2001] for further information.

When no event duration information is present in the alert message that is sent to the correlation system, the end time of the event is assumed to be identical to its start time. When duration information is available, the correlation system can easily calculate the end time by adding this duration to the event's start time.

2.2   Determining the Alert's Source and Target

When the timestamps have been set (using any of the techniques described above), the source(s) and target(s) of the attack have to be determined. According to the IDMEF standard, the attack source is composed of information about the node, the user, the process, and the network service that originated the attack. The attack target also includes a list of affected files. Not all fields have to be defined for both the source and the target, but the correlation system requires at least one non-empty field for each.

When the correlation system receives alert message with empty source or target attributes, the preprocessing phase has to provide some best-effort values. For host-based alerts, the node fields of the attacks' source and target are set to the address of the host where the sensor is located. For network-based alerts, the node information is taken from the source and destination IP addresses.

2.3   Determining the Attack's Name

Finally, an alert can be augmented with additional information on the basis of the standardized alert name that is assigned in the previous phase. An example for such information is the attack class, which describes the type of an attack with respect to a simple scheme that distinguishes between local or remote information gathering and privilege escalation attempts. The class information is useful because it allows one to group together similar attacks.

ID	Name	Sensor	Start/End	Source	Target	Tag
1	IIS Exploit	N1	12.0 / 12.0	80.0.0.1	10.0.0.1, port:80	
2	Portscan	N2	10.1 / 14.8	31.3.3.7	10.0.0.1	
3	Portscan	N1	10.0 / 15.0	31.3.3.7	10.0.0.1	
4	Apache Exploit	N1	22.0 / 22.0	31.3.3.7	10.0.0.1, port:80	
5	Bad Request	A	22.1 / 22.1	**10.0.0.1**	**10.0.0.1**, Apache	
6	Local Exploit	H	24.6 / 24.6	**10.0.0.1**	**10.0.0.1**, linuxconf	
7	Local Exploit	H	24.7 / 24.7	**10.0.0.1**	**10.0.0.1**, linuxconf	

Table 4.2. Alert Preprocessing

In our example scenario, the three alerts reported by the host- and application-based sensors do not contain any information about the attack's source and target. Therefore, appropriate best-effort values are supplied during the preprocessing step. Table 4.2 shows the results after the last three alerts were augmented with additional values.

Chapter 5

ALERT AGGREGATION AND VERIFICATION

After the alert collection steps, a stream of alerts in a suitable format is available and the correlation process can start with the actual identification of higher-level structures. This process follows a hierarchical structure. In the beginning, only alerts that are closely related to each other are merged into meta-alerts. At this level of abstraction, the alerts that are considered for merging have to possess a strong temporal and spatial proximity. In later phases of the correlation process, the proximity requirements are relaxed. Meta-Alerts at the lower abstraction layers in the hierarchy are merged into larger building blocks that are subsequently used as input for correlation at the next abstraction layer.

This chapter introduces the correlation steps in the lower level of the hierarchy. Starting from alert fusion (a step that identifies alerts that refer to the same underlying event), we introduce the correlation phases that deal with alerts that are in a close temporal and spatial relationship. Then, Chapter 6 will deal with the extraction of higher-level structures that connect incidents that occur at different locations in the network and possible ways to recognize a sequence of actions that a malicious attacker performs to reach particular goals.

1. Alert Fusion

The task of the alert fusion phase is to combine alerts that result from the independent detection of the same attack occurrence by different intrusion detection systems. Alert fusion acts as a filter that removes obvious duplicates from the correlation process. Note that the terminology that is introduced in this book occasionally differs from terminology used by other researchers in the field. Intrusion detection and especially alert correlation are new and evolving areas of active research and for many terms no generally agreed upon definitions exist. It is the hope of the authors that this book might aid in establishing a common language for the different phases of the alert correlation process.

The decision to fuse two alerts in the alert fusion step is based on the temporal difference between these two alerts and the information that they contain. The alert fusion phase only considers two alerts as candidates for fusion when their start times and end times differ by less than a certain, predefined time span t. It is not required that two alerts have identical time values in order to compensate for clock drift when sensors are located at different machines and for the time it takes the alert messages to reach the correlator. In addition, it is necessary that the alerts are received from different sensors. This is reasonable because it cannot be expected that a certain sensor emits two similar alerts with different time stamps for one single attack occurrence. Finally, all overlapping attributes (i.e., attributes for which both alerts specify values) have to be identical. There are no restrictions on the values of attributes that are only specified by a single alert. At a first glance, these constraints seem very restrictive. However, the purpose of the fusion phase is to combine duplicate alerts, not to correlate closely related attacks (this is implemented in later phases).

When two alerts are fused, the resulting meta-alert is assigned the earlier of both start times and end times. This is done in the assumption that both alerts are related to the same attack, and a later time stamp is likely to be the result of delays at the sensors. Because the values of attributes that are defined in both alerts have to be identical, the corresponding attributes of the meta-alert receive the same values. For attributes that are only defined in a single alert, the corresponding attributes of the meta-alert are assigned the respective values that are defined. An alternative way of describing the attributes of the meta-alert after fusing two alerts is that the attribute fields of the fused meta-alert are set to the union of the values of the respective alert attributes.

Note that it is possible that multiple sensor alerts are fused into a single meta-alert. In this case, two alerts are first fused into a meta-alert that is subsequently fused (one at a time) with additional sensor alerts.

Equation 5.1 defines alert fusion more formally as a function f on two alerts A_1 and A_2 such that

$$f(A_1, A_2) = A_{12} \quad \text{with} \quad \begin{aligned} &A_{12}.\text{start time} = \min(A_1.\text{start time}, A_2.\text{start time}), \\ &A_{12}.\text{end time} = \min(A_1.\text{end time}, A_2.\text{end time}), \\ &\forall_{\text{other attributes a}} : \; A_{12}.\text{a} = A_1.\text{a} \bigcup A_2.\text{a} \end{aligned}$$

$$\text{if } (|A_1.\text{start time} - A_2.\text{start time}| < t \; \wedge \; |A_1.\text{end time} - A_2.\text{end time}| < t \; \wedge$$
$$A_1.\text{sensor} \neq A_2.\text{sensor} \; \wedge$$
$$\forall_{\text{all other attributes a defined in both } A_1 \text{ and } A_2} : \; A_1.\text{a} = A_2.\text{a})$$

$$\tag{5.1}$$

The two alerts that refer to the portscan attack in the example scenario (Alert 2, Alert 3) can be fused because their start times and end times are close in time and all remaining fields are identical. Note that the two alerts referring to the local exploit (Alert 6, Alert 7) cannot be fused because both are produced by the same sensor.

ID	Name	Sensor	Start/End	Source	Target	Tag
1	IIS Exploit	N1	12.0 / 12.0	80.0.0.1	10.0.0.1, port:80	
2	Portscan	N2	10.1 / 14.8	31.3.3.7	10.0.0.1	correlated
3	Portscan	N1	10.0 / 15.0	31.3.3.7	10.0.0.1	correlated
4	Apache Exploit	N1	22.0 / 22.0	31.3.3.7	10.0.0.1, port:80	
5	Bad Request	A	22.1 / 22.1		localhost, Apache	
6	Local Exploit	H	24.6 / 24.6		linuxconf	
7	Local Exploit	H	24.7 / 24.7		linuxconf	
8	**Meta-Alert**	{N1, N2}	**10.0 / 14.8**	**31.3.3.7**	**10.0.0.1**	{2, 3}

Table 5.1. Alert Fusion

The result of the alert fusion phase is shown in Table 5.1. The generated meta-alert is tagged with the references to the two alerts that were fused, while both portscan alerts are tagged as being correlated.

2. Alert Verification

An important task of alert correlation is the aggregation of alerts to provide a high-level view (i.e., the "big picture") of malicious activity on the network. Unfortunately, when the correlation process receives false positives as input, the quality of the results can degrade significantly. Correlating alerts that refer to failed attacks can easily result in the detection of whole attack scenarios that are nonexistent.

Previous work [Cuppens and Miege, 2002; Ning et al., 2002] states that alert correlation can be used both to reduce the total number of alerts and to reduce the number of false alerts. However, these approaches assume that real attacks trigger more than a single alert. As a result, the systems can focus on alert clusters and discard all alerts that have not been correlated. Unfortunately, this assumption has not be substantiated by experimental data or supported by a rigorous discussion. Consider a common situation where an attacker is not interested in a particular host but merely wants to control as many hosts as possible, for example, to set up a distributed denial of service attack. In this case, attackers often use tools that just execute a certain canned attack against a vulnerable service. The attack either fails and the attacker moves on, or it succeeds and the intruder is granted access. In this case, no reconnaissance activity precedes the actual attack, and there is also no attempt of trying different attack vectors against a single target. Sometimes, the attacker has to send only a single packet to compromise a host. For example, the Slammer Worm [Moore et al., 2003] sends only a single UDP packet of 376 bytes to infect a victim.

In this case, it is not reasonable to assume that an intrusion detection system generates several alerts can can be correlated later. Nevertheless, a successful intrusion has occurred.

We claim that the reduction of false alerts is an important *prerequisite* to achieve good correlation results instead of an outcome of the correlation process itself. Also, a recent paper [Ning and Xu, 2003] on alert correlation mentions that "false alerts generated by IDSs have a negative impact." Therefore, we introduce an alert verification phase that attempts to remove (or tag) alerts that do not represent successful attacks.

When a sensor outputs an alert, there are three possibilities:

1 The sensor has correctly identified a successful attack. This alert is most likely relevant (i.e., a true positive).

2 The sensor has correctly identified an attack, but the attack failed to meet its objectives. Although some sites might be interested in failed attack attempts, the alert should be differentiated from a successful instance. This kind of alert is called a irrelevant positive or nontextual (reflecting the missing contextual information that the IDS would require to determine a failed attack).

3 The sensor incorrectly identified an event as an attack. The alert represents incorrect information (i.e., a false positive).

The idea of alert verification is to discriminate between successful and failed intrusion attempts (both false and irrelevant positives). This is important for the correlation process because although a failed attack indicates malicious intent, it does not provide increased privileges or any additional information (besides the fact that an attacker learned that the particular attack is ineffective).

In our example scenario, the alert corresponding to the worm attack (Alert 1) is identified as being unsuccessful because it is a Microsoft IIS exploit that targets a Linux service. Thus, the alert is being tagged as irrelevant and excluded from further correlation, as shown in Table 5.2.

There are different techniques that can be used to perform alert verification. One possibility is to compare the configuration of the victim machine (e.g., operating system, running services, service version) to the requirements of a successful attack. When the victim is not vulnerable to a particular attack (because the configuration does not satisfy the attack requirements), then the alert can be tagged as failed. For example, a certain exploit might require that the victim is running a vulnerable version of a Microsoft IIS server. When the victim's configuration shows that it is running an Apache server on Linux, the exploit cannot succeed.

Another possibility is to model the expected "outcome" of attacks. The "outcome" describes the visible and checkable traces that a certain attack leaves

ID	Name	Sensor	Start/End	Source	Target	Tag
1	IIS Exploit	N1	12.0 / 12.0	80.0.0.1	10.0.0.1, port:80	**irrelevant**
2	Scanning	N2	10.1 / 14.8	31.3.3.7	10.0.0.1	
3	Portscan	N1	10.0 / 15.0	31.3.3.7	10.0.0.1	
4	Apache Exploit	N1	22.0 / 22.0	31.3.3.7	10.0.0.1, port:80	
5	Bad Request	A	22.1 / 22.1		localhost, Apache	
6	Local Exploit	H	24.6 / 24.6		linuxconf	
7	Local Exploit	H	24.7 / 24.7		linuxconf	
8	Meta-Alert	{N1, N2}	10.0 / 14.8	31.3.3.7	10.0.0.1	{2, 3}

Table 5.2. Alert Verification

at a host or on the network (e.g., a temporary file or an outgoing network connection). When an alert has to be verified, the system can check for these traces.

An important distinction between different alert verification mechanisms is whether they are *active* or *passive*. Active verification mechanisms are defined as mechanisms that gather configuration data or forensic traces after an alert occurs. Passive mechanisms, on the other hand, gather configuration data once (or at regular, scheduled intervals) and have data available before the attack occurs. Both active and passive techniques can be used to check attack requirements against victim configurations. To check for traces that might be left after an attack, only active mechanisms can be employed. Note that the distinction between active and passive mechanisms is solely based on the *point in time* when the configuration or forensic data is collected. Passive mechanisms perform this task before an alert is received, active mechanisms perform it as a reaction to a received alert.

The most important requirement for the alert verification process is *accuracy*. An accurate verification process will keep the number of false negatives (i.e., an alert is marked as irrelevant, when in fact it is) and false positives (i.e., an alert is marked as relevant, although it is not) low. There are different factors that influence accuracy. One factor is the quality of the data that is gathered, another factor is its timeliness. Both factors are critical; it is not sufficient to have high quality data that is out of date, but it is also unsatisfactory when incorrect data is collected.

Another requirement is a low cost of the verification process, where cost is measured along two axes. One axis reflects the cost of deploying and maintaining the alert verification system. The other axis reflects the costs of impact of the verification process on the normal operation of the network. This cost includes whether it necessary to shut down regular network operations to perform alert verification, or whether the alert verification process has adverse effects on the running services.

In the following, we describe the different ways to verify the success of attacks in more detail and highlight the individual advantages and disadvantages. Note that the following description present individual approaches. However, it is possible and common to combine techniques to compensate for drawbacks of individual techniques and to combine their advantages.

2.1 Passive Approach

As mentioned above, passive verification mechanisms depend on *a priori* gathered information about the hosts, the network topology, and the installed services. A description of the network installation is required and can be, for example, specified in a formal model such as M2D2 [Morin et al., 2002].

Given an alert, it is possible to verify whether the target of the attack exists and whether a (potentially vulnerable) service is running. For remote attacks, it is also possible to check whether malicious packets can possibly reach the target, given the network topology and the firewall rule configuration, or whether the target host reassembles the packets as expected by the intruder (e.g., using the tool by Shankar and Paxson [Shankar and Paxson, 2003]).

The advantage of passive mechanisms is the fact that they do not interfere with the normal operation of the network. In addition, it is not necessary to perform additional tests that delay the notification of administrators or the start of active countermeasures. A disadvantage of passive mechanisms are potential differences between the state stored in the knowledge base and the actual security status of the network. New services might have been installed or the firewall rules might have been changed without updating the knowledge base. This can lead to attacks that are tagged as irrelevant, even though a vulnerable target exists. Another disadvantage is the limitation of the type of information that can be gathered in advance. When the signature of an attack is matched against a packet sent to a vulnerable target, the attack could still fail for a number of other reasons (e.g., incorrect offset for a buffer overflow exploit). To increase the confidence in verification results, it is often required to actively check audit data recorded at the victim machine.

2.2 Active Approach

Active alert verification mechanisms do not rely on *a priori* gathered information. Instead, the verification process actively initiates the information gathering process when an alert is received. This information gathering process can check the current configuration of the victim host or scan for attack traces.

Active with remote access

Mechanisms in this group require that a network connection can be established to the victim machine. One active verification mechanism with remote access is based on the use of vulnerability scanners. A vulnerability scanner is a program specifically designed to search a given target (piece of software, computer, network, etc.) for weaknesses. The scanner systematically engages the target in an attempt to assess where the target is vulnerable to certain known attacks. When an attack has been detected, a scanner can be used to check for the vulnerability that this attack attempts to exploit. Note that a vulnerability scanner could also be used in a passive setup. In this case, the full range of scans would be run in advance (or in regular intervals).

A network connection permits scanning of the attack target and allows one to assess whether a target service is still responding or whether it has become unresponsive. It also enables the alert verification system to check whether unknown ports accept connections, which could be evidence that a backdoor is installed. In this case, however, care must be taken to prevent false positives that stem from dynamically allocated ports. To this end, one could use blacklists of well-known backdoor ports, whitelists that specify port ranges for well-known applications (e.g., X servers), or service fingerprinting to detect legitimate applications. Also, the active verification system can keep a list of applications that were found running during the last scan and raise an alert when this list changes.

Active alert verification has the advantage, compared to passive mechanisms, that the information is current. This allows one to assess the status of the target host and the attacked service and to recognize changes at the victim host that serve as an indication of an attack.

Although the information is current, however, it might not be completely accurate. One has to consider that a vulnerability scanner can also have false positives and false negatives. When an alert is verified, if the vulnerability scanner determines that the service is vulnerable when in fact it is not, the alert is simply reported by the IDS. In this case, the alert is a false positive (because the service is not vulnerable) and the verification mechanism has failed. However, the security of the system is not affected, and without verification, the alert would have been reported as well. A more significant problem are false negatives. In this case, a valid alert is suppressed because the vulnerability scanner determines that the target is not vulnerable when in fact, it is. Although such a scenario is very undesirable, it is not very likely to occur frequently. The reason is that a vulnerability scanner actually launches a basic instance of the attack. When this attack fails, it is very improbable that a more sophisticated instance succeeds.

Another drawback is the fact that active actions are visible on the network and it is possible that scanning has an adverse effect on one's own machines. Port scanning consumes network bandwidth and resources at the scanned host. To minimize the impact on a operational network, results can be cached for some time. This is especially important when an intruder runs scripts that repeat the same attack with different parameters. Note, however, that caching involves a tradeoff between resource usage and accuracy. When results are cached too long, the advantage of active verification is reduced. As scans are only initiated on a per-alert base, it is not necessary to run all tests that a vulnerability scanner includes, but at most a single one for each alert (minus those for which cached results are available).

In addition, tests run by a vulnerability scanner might crash a service. A vulnerability scanner can perform tests in a *nonintrusive* or in an *intrusive* manner. When running nonintrusive tests, a vulnerability is not actually exploited, but inferred from the type and version of a running service (e.g., by analyzing banner information). When running an intrusive test, the vulnerability is actually exploited. While this delivers more accurate results, it often results in the crash or disruption of the victim service. Sometimes, the crash of a service process can be tolerated, for example, when the service is implemented using multiple threads (such as Apache's thread pool). In this case, the failure of a single thread does not have a negative impact, because the other threads still serve requests. In addition, the failed thread is automatically restarted after a short period of time. On the other hand, when the crash of a service process interrupts the whole service, then the corresponding test should be excluded altogether from the active verification process. This also helps to prevent a possible attack where an attacker triggers an alert to have the alert verification system check and subsequently crash the service. The problem of selecting the appropriate tests is a result of the conflict between the goal of getting accurate results and the goal of having minimal impact on the operational network. While intrusive tests are more reliable in obtaining proper results, the risk of affecting services is greater.

Note that the alert verification mechanism should only be used to check alerts raised by packets that can possibly reach their destination. That is, the intrusion detection system (together with the alert verification system) should be located behind a firewall. This makes sure that only relevant packets are scanned for attacks by the IDS and later verified. Otherwise, an attacker could potentially bypass the firewall and launch attacks by means of the alert verification system.

The scope of remote scans is also limited, in that the identification of some evidence associated with an attack might require local access to the victim machine. In addition, one has to make sure that the alerts generated in response to the activity of the vulnerability scanner are excluded from the correlation process.

Active with authenticated access

Mechanisms in this group gather evidence about the result of an attack using authenticated access to the victim host. The difference with respect to the previous group of techniques is the fact that the alert verification system presents authentication credentials to the target host.

Active verification with authenticated access can be implemented by creating dedicated user accounts with appropriate privilege settings at the target machines. The alert verification system can then remotely log in and execute scripts or system commands. This allows one to monitor the integrity of system files (e.g., the password file or system specific binaries) or check for well-known files that are created by attacks (e.g., worms usually leave an executable copy of the worm on the file system). In addition, programs that retrieve interesting forensic data such as open network connections (such as netstat), open files (such as lsof) or running processes (such as ps) can be invoked.

The advantage of mechanisms in this group is the access to high-quality data gathered directly from a target machine. One downside is the need to configure each machine for authenticated remote access. This might be cumbersome in large network installations or when hosts with many different operating systems are used. On the other hand, in large networks, such accounts may already exist for maintenance purposes and can be also used for gathering of forensic evidence. Another problem is the fact that the information provided by general user-space tools might not be as complete and accurate as it is possible with specialized, often kernel-space tools.

Active with dedicated sensor support

Mechanisms in this group require, in addition to authenticated access, special auditing support installed at the target machines. This auditing support can be operating system extensions or special purpose tools, such as host-based intrusion detection systems. The differences between using standard tools and relying on dedicated sensors is that standard tools are common in most distributions. In addition, dedicated sensors often need complex configuration.

Dedicated sensors can be used to monitor system calls issued by user applications. This allows one to check for the spawning of suspicious processes (e.g., shell invocations) or for accesses to critical files. As opposed to standard tools that present a current snapshot of the system, sensors can keep a record of malicious activity. This enables the verification system to gather events that are only visible for a short period of time, which could be missed by a snapshot.

The advantage of dedicated sensor support is the ability to provide the most detailed and accurate audit records. The drawback is the effort required to install and configure these sensors, and the fact that certain sensors are not available for all platforms.

General issues of active verification

One issue that affects all active verification mechanisms is the problem that information is gathered directly from the victim machine. It can be argued that an attacker can tamper with the compromised system to eliminate suspicious traces or, at least, hide her activity from the auditing system. This is particularly true when the information is gathered remotely (e.g., using a vulnerability scanner).

There are different approaches to addressing this problem. One possibility is to operate in a best-effort mode and attempt to scan the potential victim host as fast as possible after the alert is received. This, of course, offers a small window of vulnerability that can be exploited by the attacker. A more secure option is to delay packets that have raised an alert until the verification mechanism has finished. This makes sure that the victim host has not been compromised by this attack, but it requires an in-line intrusion detection system.

Another option can be used when data is directly gathered on the victim machines via scripts or dedicated sensors. Here, audit tools should be run at least with privileges that require administrative (i.e., root) access to be turned off. This maintains the integrity of the sensor when the intruder obtains user access only or manages to crash a service with a denial of service attack. The sensors operate in a best-effort mode and deliver accurate results as long as possible. Also, simply disabling auditing is a suspicious action by itself. A more secure option is the use of a more restrictive access control system such as LIDS [LIDS, 2004] or Security-Enhanced Linux [Loscocco and Smalley, 2001]. These systems can prevent the administrator from interfering with the audit facility such that physical access to the machine is required to change or disable security settings.

3.   Attack Thread Reconstruction

An attack thread combines a series of alerts that refer to attacks launched by one attacker against a single target. This is similar to the concept of an *alert thread* in Emerald [Porras and Neumann, 1997; Neumann and Porras, 1999], which is defined as a series of alerts from a single sensor that refer to the same attack, possibly separated in time. Different from Emerald's alert thread mechanism, our thread reconstruction technique allows alerts to be from different sensors.

The goal of this phase is to correlate alerts that are caused by an attacker that tests different exploits against a certain program or that runs the same exploit multiple times to guess correct values for certain parameters (e.g., the offsets and memory addresses for a buffer overflow). The correlation process still operates on very basic relationships between alerts. At this level, we do not consider alerts that are caused by multiple intruders that cooperate to attack a single target. Also, we do not relate different steps of a complete attack scenario. The task of attack thread recognition is limited to the aggregation of alerts that are caused by the activity of a single attacker who focuses on a single target.

Alert threads are constructed by merging alerts with equivalent source and target attributes that occur in a certain temporal proximity. Attacks are considered to occur in sequence after each other, and therefore, it is not necessary that both start times and end times of the alerts are close (as was required for alert fusion). Instead, the requirement is that the end time of the earlier attack has to be close to the start time of the following one. There are no additional constraints on any other attributes. Alert thread reconstruction is defined as a function f on two alerts A_1 and A_2 (shown in Equation 5.2) such that

$$f(A_1, A_2) = A_{12} \quad \text{with} \quad \begin{aligned} & A_{12}.\text{start time} = \min(A_1.\text{start time}, A_2.\text{start time}), \\ & A_{12}.\text{end time} = \max(A_1.\text{end time}, A_2.\text{end time}), \\ & \forall_{\text{other attributes a}} : \ A_{12}.\text{a} = A_1.\text{a} \bigcup A_2.\text{a} \end{aligned} \quad (5.2)$$

$$\text{if } (|A_1.\text{start time} - A_2.\text{end time}| < t \ \lor \ |A_2.\text{start time} - A_1.\text{end time}| < t) \ \land$$
$$\forall_{\text{source and target attributes a defined in both } A_1 \text{ and } A_2} : \ A_1.\text{a} = A_2.\text{a}$$

In the example scenario, the meta-alert (Alert 8) that was created by fusing the two portscan alerts and the remote Apache exploit (Alert 4) are merged into one attack thread because both have the same source and target attributes and are close in time. Note that Alert 4 is not merged with the individual portscan alerts (Alert 2 or Alert 3). This is because Alert 8, which is the meta-alert summarizing Alert 2 and Alert 3, has already been used for the merging process (as explained in Chapter 3). Also, the two alerts referring to the local exploit (Alert 6 and Alert 7) are combined in one attack thread. Table 5.3 shows the alerts that are created or modified in the alert thread reconstruction phase.

4. Attack Session Reconstruction

The attack session reconstruction phase attempts to link network-based to host-based alerts. Linking network-based to host-based alerts is difficult because the information that is present in these alerts differs. Network-based sensors can provide the source and destination IP addresses and ports of packet(s) that contain detected attacks. Host-based sensors, on the other hand, include information about the process that is attacked and the user on whose behalf this process is executed. Because it is not straightforward to relate network-based information (IP addresses and ports) to host-based information (process and user identifiers), it is not obvious how a connection between alerts from intrusion detection sensors operating on different event streams can be established.

One approach is to require a rough spatial and temporal correspondence of the alerts. The idea is that a host-based alert should be linked to a network-

ID	Name	Sensor	Start/End	Source	Target	Tag
1	IIS Exploit	N1	12.0 / 12.0	80.0.0.1	10.0.0.1, port:80	
2	Scanning	N2	10.1 / 14.8	31.3.3.7	10.0.0.1	
3	Portscan	N1	10.0 / 15.0	31.3.3.7	10.0.0.1	
4	Apache Exploit	N1	22.0 / 22.0	31.3.3.7	10.0.0.1, port:80	correlated
5	Bad Request	A	22.1 / 22.1		localhost, Apache	
6	Local Exploit	H	24.6 / 24.6	10.0.0.1	10.0.0.1, linuxconf	correlated
7	Local Exploit	H	24.7 / 24.7	10.0.0.1	10.0.0.1, linuxconf	correlated
8	Meta-Alert	{N1, N2}	10.0 / 14.8	31.3.3.7	10.0.0.1	{2, 3} correlated
9	**Meta-Alert**	**{N1, N2}**	**10.0 / 22.0**	**31.3.3.7**	**10.0.0.1, port:80**	**{4, 8}**
10	**Meta-Alert**	**H**	**24.6 / 24.7**	**10.0.0.1**	**10.0.0.1, linuxconf**	**{6, 7}**

Table 5.3. Attack Thread Reconstruction

based alert when the host-based attack occurs a short time after the network-based attack and the network-based attack targets the host where the host-based attack is observed. This approach is simple, but has the obvious drawback that it is very imprecise and might correlate independent alerts. It can, however, be improved by utilizing *a priori* information about the port(s) used by a certain network service. For example, by modeling the fact that a web server process listens on port 80, host-based alerts referring to this process are only correlated to network-based alerts with destination port 80 on the host where the web server is running. Another possibility is to specify that a certain attack is known to *prepare for* or *to be a precondition for* another attack. This allows a packet containing a known web-based attack to be linked to an alert raised by a sensor monitoring the victim web server. To the best of our knowledge, all current alert correlation systems require such information, manually encoded in a knowledge base (called preconditions and postconditions in [Cuppens and Miege, 2002] and prerequisites and consequences in [Ning et al., 2002]).

We argue that it is useful to extend these manually defined links between network-based and host-based alerts with a more general and automatic mechanism. This mechanism is based on information (i) about the network port(s) that processes are bound to and (ii) about the parent-child relationships between processes. Given this information, it is possible to determine whether it is likely that data that triggers a network-based alert reaches the victim process reported in a host-based alert. This can be done by linking a network-based alert to a host-based alert when the victim process or one of its ancestors listens to the destination port mentioned in the network-based alert. It is necessary to include the ancestor processes because network daemons often fork child processes to service each single request. In this case, a child process may be reported as the victim in the host-based alert, and it is its parent who is listening to the network port mentioned in the network-based alert.

Equation 5.3 shows the definition for attack session reconstruction as a function f on two alerts A_1 and A_2. Without loss of generality, it is assumed that A_1 is the network-based alert that precedes the host-based alert A_2.

$$f(A_1, A_2) = A_{12} \quad \text{with} \quad \begin{aligned} & A_{12}.\text{start time} = \min(A_1.\text{start time}, A_2.\text{start time}), \\ & A_{12}.\text{end time} = \max(A_1.\text{end time}, A_2.\text{end time}), \\ & \forall_{\text{other attributes a}} : A_{12}.\text{a} = A_1.\text{a} \bigcup A_2.\text{f} \end{aligned} \quad (5.3)$$

$$\text{if} \ (|A_2.\text{start time} - A_1.\text{end time}| < t \ \wedge \exists A_1.\text{target.port} \ \wedge \\ \exists A_2.\text{target.process} \ \wedge A_2.\text{target.process linked to } A_1.\text{target.port})$$

One possible solution to gather the necessary *links-to* information needed for attack session reconstruction is a host-based sensor that periodically takes a snapshot of all active processes with their parents and a snapshot of the connections between processes and network ports. These snapshots can be consulted when a host-based alert is reported shortly after a network-based alert. In this case, the destination port of the network connection that is responsible for the alert is retrieved from the corresponding network-based alert. Then, the process that accepted the network connection at this destination port can be determined. Finally, it is checked whether the victim process reported in the host-based alert is a child of the process that accepted the network connection. If so, both alerts are combined into a single attack session.

This technique is not perfect and might miss certain attack sessions. For example, it is possible that data is exchanged between two processes when one process is not the direct descendant of the other process (e.g., using the file system or local UNIX sockets). With the simple snapshot-based sensor, such data flow cannot be tracked because only ancestor/descendant relationships are considered. Another shortcoming is the fact that extremely short-lived events might be lost. Consider a process that is created in response to a network request. This process might exit or crash before a snapshot is taken. In this case, even though a proper host-based alert might be created, the correlation system lacks the information about the process and its parent.

The drawbacks could be mitigated by including process tracing support into the operating system kernel. Instead of periodically pulling information from the kernel, a kernel-level sensor can push information about process creation and read or write operations to the correlation system when these events occur.

In our example attack scenario, the host-based sensor on the Linux host detects that Apache listens on port 80. This allows the session reconstruction to link the application-based alert (Alert 5) to the meta-alert describing the remote exploit (Alert 9), creating a new meta-alert as shown in Table 5.4.

ID	Name	Sensor	Start/End	Source	Target	Tag
1	IIS Exploit	N1	12.0 / 12.0	80.0.0.1	10.0.0.1, port:80	
2	Scanning	N2	10.1 / 14.8	31.3.3.7	10.0.0.1	
3	Portscan	N1	10.0 / 15.0	31.3.3.7	10.0.0.1	
4	Apache Exp.	N1	22.0 / 22.0	31.3.3.7	10.0.0.1, port:80	
5	Bad Request	A	22.1 / 22.1	10.0.0.1	10.0.0.1, Apache	correlated
6	Local Exploit	H	24.6 / 24.6		linuxconf	
7	Local Exploit	H	24.7 / 24.7		linuxconf	
8	Meta-Alert	{N1, N2}	10.0 / 14.8	31.3.3.7	10.0.0.1	{2, 3}
9	Meta-Alert	{N1, N2}	10.0 / 22.0	31.3.3.7	10.0.0.1, port:80	{4, 8} correlated
10	Meta-Alert	H	24.6 / 24.7	10.0.0.1	10.0.0.1, linuxconf	{6, 7}
11	**Meta-Alert**	**{N1, N2, A}**	**10.0 / 22.1**	**{31.3.3.7, 10.0.0.1}**	**10.0.0.1, port:80, Apache**	**{5, 9}**

Table 5.4. Attack Session Reconstruction

5.   Attack Focus Recognition

The task of the attack focus recognition phase is to identify hosts that are either the source or the target of a substantial amount of attacks. This phase aggregates the alerts associated with a single host attacking multiple victims (called a *one2many* scenario) and multiple attackers attacking a single victim (called a *many2one* scenario).

The attack focus phase is effective in reducing the number of alerts caused by (distributed) denial of service (DDoS) attacks and portscan activity. In general, alerts related to a DDoS attempt can be merged into a single many2one meta-alert, while alerts related to portscans are combined into a single one2many meta-alert.

Attack focus recognition is, in its simplest form, based on a sliding time window. The correlation system computes the total number of attacks that each host has launched during a time window w. Each host that is responsible for more that than a certain number of attacks (given by an *a priori* threshold t) is considered to perform a one2many attack and an appropriate meta-alert is created.

A one2many alert can be further classified as a *horizontal portscan* or as a *horizontal multiscan*. A horizontal portscan refers to a situation where a certain host probes the status of a particular port on many targets. A horizontal multiscan is similar, but instead of a single port, multiple ports are probed on each host. Note that the set of probed ports is consistent between targets. To further classify a one2many alert as one of these two types of scans, the destination ports of the individual attacks are analyzed. When all attacks target the same port, or the same set of ports, the alert is further classified as either a horizontal portscan or a horizontal multiscan.

In addition to the number of attacks that each host has launched, the total number of times that each host was the victim of an attack is determined as well. When a host is the victim of more than a certain number of attacks, an appropriate many2one meta-alert is created. When the number of attacks against the host exceeds a second threshold, which is significantly higher than the threshold necessary to create a many2one alert, the meta-alert is additionally tagged as a denial of service.

The source field of a one2many meta-alert is set to be the attacker's host, while the target and all other remaining fields are the union of the targets of the individual attacks. The many2one scenario operates in a similar way, the only difference being that the roles of the attacker (source) and victim (target) are reversed.

More complex forms of portscan detection are possible, especially against an attacker who uses multiple machines to scan a small number of ports on multiple targets. In this case, the amount of attacks from each attacking machine is not enough to trigger a one2many alert, and each victim host receives too few scans to trigger a many2one alert. Another obvious attack against a simple time-window-based approach are *stealth scans*. These are scans that are deliberately executed very slow so that the number of attacks in each time window is smaller than the threshold necessary to trigger a meta-alert.

Spice (Stealthy Portscan and Intrusion Correlation Engine) [Staniford et al., 2000], which was developed by Silicon Defense, attempts to solve the problem of slow scans by using an adaptive time window. A preprocessing step labels anomalous packets as suspicious and increases the time windows for these packets. This allows Spice to purge information about irrelevant packets early and only store potential attacks. Because less packets need to be stored, the time window can be increased. The performance of Spice naturally depends on the quality of the preprocessing step. When attack packets are not recognized as such, the later phases cannot identify any attacks.

In our example scenario, attack focus recognition cannot be applied to the alerts. Note, however, that if several portscan alerts against multiple targets from the same source were received, these alerts would be merged into a one2many meta-alert.

Chapter 6

HIGH-LEVEL ALERT STRUCTURES

This chapter addresses the problems of identifying higher-level structures that connect incidents that occur at different locations in the network and possible ways to recognize a sequence of actions that a malicious attacker performs to reach particular goals. Also, the analysis of the impact of an attack on a network and its services is discussed. Finally, we briefly mention the problem of data anonymization when correlation is performed between sites that do not completely trust each other.

1. Multistep Correlation

Multistep correlation is used to identify high-level attack patterns that are composed of several individual attacks. Usually, these high-level patterns are defined by using some form of expert knowledge. Consider, for example, an *island-hop* scenario. This scenario models an attacker who breaks into a host and then uses that host as a platform to break into other hosts. The scenario is able to identify chains of alerts where the victim referenced in one alert becomes the attacker in the following one. Another example of a multistep scenario is an attack where an intruder first scans a victim host, then breaks into a user account on that host, and finally escalates her privileges to become the root user.

Multistep correlation can be also used as an alert verification technique at a higher level. In this case, scenarios to recognize patterns that are known to be irrelevant are specified. This allows one to filter out sequences of events that should be discarded (e.g., in case of a worm that incessantly probes for multiple vulnerabilities known to be patched).

The specification of multistep attacks is usually written by a domain expert using an attack specification language. One example of an attack specification language is STATL [Eckmann et al., 2002]. STATL is an extensible attack specification language which is interpreted by the corresponding runtime, the STAT core.

The STATL language provides constructs to represent an attack as a composition of *states* and *transitions*. States are used to characterize different snapshots of a system during the evolution of an attack. Obviously, it is not feasible to represent the complete state of a system (e.g., volatile memory, file system); therefore, a STATL scenario uses variables to record just those parts of the system state that are needed to define an attack signature (e.g., the value of a counter or the source IP address of network packet). A transition has an associated *action* that is a specification of the event that can cause the scenario to move to a new state. An example for an action could be the opening of a TCP connection. The space of possible relevant actions is constrained by a *transition assertion*, which is a filter condition on the events that can possibly match the action. For example, an assertion can require that a TCP connection be opened with a specific destination port.

It is possible for several occurrences of the same attack to be active at the same time. A STATL attack scenario, therefore, has an operational semantics in terms of a set of *instances* of the same scenario *specification*. The scenario specification represents the scenario's definition and global environment, and a scenario instance represents a particular attack that is currently in progress. The evolution of the set of instances of a scenario is determined by the type of transitions in the scenario definition. A transition can be *nonconsuming*, *consuming*, or *unwinding*.

A nonconsuming transition is used to represent a step of an occurring attack that does not prevent further occurrences of attacks from spawning from the transition's source state. Therefore, when a nonconsuming transition is taken, the source state remains valid, and the destination state becomes valid, too. For example, if a multistep attack consists of the two steps that are the uploading of a file to a web server though FTP followed by an HTTP request for that file, then the second step does not invalidate the previous state. That is, another HTTP request for the same file can occur. Semantically, the firing of a nonconsuming transition causes the creation of a new scenario instance. The original instance is still in the original state, while the new instance is in the state that is the destination state of the transition taken. In contrast, the firing of a consuming transition makes the source state of a particular attack occurrence invalid. Semantically, the firing of a consuming transition does not generate a new scenario instance; it simply changes the state of the original one.

Unwinding transitions represent a form of "rollback", and they are used to describe events and conditions that can invalidate the progress of one or more scenario instances and require the return to an earlier state. For example, the deletion of a file can invalidate a condition needed for an attack to complete, and, therefore, a corresponding scenario instance can be brought back to a previous state, such as before the file was created. For details about the semantics of the STATL language, see [Eckmann et al., 2002].

Systems, such as STAT, that use state-transitions to represent intrusions, or similar systems that use equally powerful specification techniques such as petri nets [Kumar and Spafford, 1994] or rules [Porras and Neumann, 1997], allow one to specify arbitrary attack scenarios. An advantage of modeling complete scenarios is the fact that it is possible to monitor, in real time, the evolution of a particular scenario instance from state to state, possibly anticipating the further progress of an intrusion, in order to prepare or invoke appropriate countermeasures.

However, it is required to explicitly encode each attack scenario, and in particular, each venue that an attacker can take to progress to the next step. This can be cumbersome and error prone, as certain aspects of the attack could be overlooked. Much recent work on alert correlation has focused on multi-step correlation to reduce the amount of knowledge that needs to be explicitly encoded.

The proposed approaches are based on pre- and postconditions [Cuppens and Miege, 2002] or prerequisites and consequences [Ning et al., 2002] of individual attack steps and do not require complete scenarios to be modeled explicitly.

A precondition of an attack is a necessary condition for the attack to be successful. For example, two preconditions for a successful local attack are the fact that the attacker has local access and the fact that a vulnerable service is running. The postcondition of an attack describes a property or a state of the system that is the immediate cause of the attack. For example, the postcondition of a successful remote buffer overflow is the fact that the attacker has local access to the machine that runs the vulnerable service. The key idea of approaches that are based on pre- and postcondition is that postconditions of certain attacks can be used as preconditions for other attacks, in the assumption that the attacker achieves a particular goal by executing a series of steps that work towards that goal.

The multistep correlation phase operates by linking an alert to a later alert when the postcondition of the first alert is a necessary precondition for the second alert *and* this precondition was not satisfied before the first alert. This means that the attack that corresponds to the first alert renders the attack that corresponds to the second alert possible. Based on the assumption of the goal-oriented intruder, the system concludes that the first attack has been carried out in order to allow the second attack.

An advantage of this technique is that it is only necessary to specify properties (that is, pre- and postconditions) for individual attacks. From these basic building blocks, arbitrary complex scenarios can be created automatically by the correlation analysis. In addition, it might also be possible to deduce "missing" attacks. Consider the situation where the correlation system receives a first series of alerts that leads to a certain system state. Then, a second series of alerts is received, but this series cannot be connected to the first one. The reason is that some precondition that is required for the first attack of the second series is not any of the postconditions of the last attack of the first series. That is, an alert is missing that could connect the first to the second series. If an attack signature exists that could connect these two series, then the multistep correlation phase might decide to connect the first to the second series regardless of a mismatch of the corresponding pre- and postconditions. The correlation system does this in the assumption that this attack has occurred, but it has not been detected by any intrusion detection system.

The problem with systems that are based on pre- and postcondition is the fact that their output is often not as easy to understand for a human operator than the output of a system that is based on models of complete attack scenarios. When a series of alerts trigger a multistep scenario, the security officer can be informed that a certain well-defined attack has been identified. The result of a system that links alerts based on pre- and postconditions, however, often produces a huge attack graph of alerts that are connected to each other, and it is not immediately obvious what happened. A solution to this problem could be the combination of both techniques. By defining common attack scenarios as attack subgraphs, the complete attack graph, which is produced by a precondition/postcondition-based system, can be searched for these subgraph patterns and a more precise report can be provided to the security officer.

ID	Name	Sensor	Start/End	Source	Target	Tag
1	IIS Exploit	N1	12.0 / 12.0	80.0.0.1	10.0.0.1, port:80	
2	Scanning	N2	10.1 / 14.8	31.3.3.7	10.0.0.1	
3	Portscan	N1	10.0 / 15.0	31.3.3.7	10.0.0.1	
4	Apache Exp.	N1	22.0 / 22.0	31.3.3.7	10.0.0.1, port:80	
5	Bad Request	A	22.1 / 22.1		localhost, Apache	
6	Local Exploit	H	24.6 / 24.6		linuxconf	
7	Local Exploit	H	24.7 / 24.7		linuxconf	
8	Meta-Alert	{N1, N2}	10.0 / 14.8	31.3.3.7	10.0.0.1	{2, 3}
9	Meta-Alert	{N1, N2}	10.0 / 22.0	31.3.3.7	10.0.0.1, port:80	{4,8}
10	Meta-Alert	H	24.6 / 24.7	10.0.0.1	10.0.0.1, linuxconf	{6, 7}, correlated
11	Meta-Alert	{N1, N2, A}	10.0 / 22.1	{31.3.3.7, 10.0.0.1}	10.0.0.1, port:80, Apache	{5, 9}, correlated
12	**Meta-Alert**	**{N1, N2, H, A}**	**10.0 / 24.7**	**{31.3.3.7, 10.0.0.1}**	**10.0.0.1, port:80, Apache, linuxconf**	**10, 11**

Table 6.1. Multistep Correlation

For our example, we assume that a multistep scenario has been defined that includes a scanning step, a break-in step, and an escalation of privileges step. Given such a scenario, the meta-alert that describes the scan and the remote attack against the web server can be merged with the local exploit. The results of this operation is shown in Table 6.1.

2. Impact Analysis

In the impact analysis phase, the effects of an attack on the proper operation of the network are determined. The idea of this phase is to analyze alerts (and the corresponding attacks) with regard to the context in which they occur. In all previous steps, alerts are evaluated independently of their environment. Only the internal information that is stored within an alert is used to determine whether it can be aggregated with others into higher-level meta-alerts. A notable exception is the alert verification phase, which includes external information to check whether it is possible for a certain attack to have succeeded or not.

The impact analysis phase relies on external information to evaluate alerts with regard to their impact on the network infrastructure and the attached resources. Information about the network and relevant resources is stored in an asset database. The asset database stores details about installed network services, dependencies between these services, and their importance to the overall operation of a network installation. An example of a dependency between two services is a mail service that requires an operational domain name service (DNS) to work properly. That is, even when the mail server itself is functional, it cannot transmit messages without being able to resolve e-mail addresses.

In the impact analysis phase, each alert is analyzed with the help of the asset database to determine which services are dependent on the attacked targets. Alerts are then augmented with this dependency information. If a status monitor that checks the operation of critical services is available, a failure of a service can be eventually linked to all alerts that could have caused the service outage.

To illustrate the way the impact analysis phase work, consider the following example. An alert is received that refers to a bandwidth denial of service attack against a particular network link. Using the asset database, the correlation system can determine that the proper operation of the domain name service is dependent on the availability of this particular link. The database also contains the information that the mail service requires an operating DNS server. When the service monitor detects a failure of the mail system (e.g., by sending messages to a test account), the failure of both the mail and DNS servers are added as additional data to the impact of the attack.

In the attack scenario that is used throughout the book, only a single service (i.e., the web server) is present, and, therefore, no dependencies are modeled in the asset database.

The impact phase can also be used to evaluate the effect of automatic response actions performed by intrusion detection systems. Traditionally, intrusion detection systems notify a human operator when an intrusion is identified. That is, the system simply displays incident data on a console, or, in urgent cases, uses alternative notification channels such as e-mail or text messages to mobile phones. However, no proactive, automatic measure is taken to prevent the intrusion.

The problem is that this opens a window of vulnerability between the point in time when the intrusion is detected and the point when the first countermeasure is launched. The size of this time window can range from seconds to hours (e.g., during nights or weekends). According to [Cohen, 1999], the success rate of an intruder rises with the time she can work undisturbed. This study reports that a skilled attacker can perform an intrusion with a 80% success rate if she is given 10 hours time before any response is launched.

Therefore, a recent trend towards intrusion *prevention* systems can be observed. These systems include automatic response systems components to choose appropriate countermeasures without human intervention. This allows to dramatically reduce the size of the vulnerability time window. Most current systems implementing automatic response mechanisms use simple decision tables to determine how to react in the case of identified attacks. More sophisticated variants such as Cooperating Security Managers [White et al., 1996] and Emerald [Porras and Neumann, 1997] use expert system techniques to analyze the attack and decide which countermeasures should be deployed.

The problem of automatic countermeasures are the adverse effects these actions may have on the usability of the network and its services. This is especially true if an attacker is able to trigger certain countermeasures on purpose to perform, for example, a denial of service attack. Consider, for example, a firewall reconfiguration which prohibits incoming connections to a certain service which is needed by users outside the network (a nightmare for e-commerce sites). Another example is the termination of processes that are considered to be responsible for malicious behavior. The problem is even exacerbated by the presence of false positives, resulting in unnecessary and adverse countermeasures.

The asset database that is used for evaluating the impact of attacks on the functioning of the network can also be used to evaluate the effect of response mechanisms [Toth and Kruegel, 2002; Balepin et al., 2004]. By taking into account the network topology and the dependencies between different services, the consequences of responses can be captured more accurately. In addition, it is possible to compare different response plans and select the one with the minimal negative impact.

3. Alert Prioritizing

Closely related to the attack's impact and the effect of a response are asset priorities. By defining appropriate priorities for one's assets, it is possible to assign higher importance to attacks that threaten more important assets.

Priorities are also important to classify alerts and quickly discard information that is irrelevant or of less importance to a particular site. The alert prioritizing phase has to take into account the security policy and the security requirements of the site where the correlation system is deployed. Therefore, there is no absolute priority of an attack. Consider, for example, a simple portscan. Scans have become so common on the Internet that most administrators consider them as mere nuisances and do not spend any time or resources in tracking down their sources. This suggests that an alert referring to a scan should be tagged with a low priority. However, the situation is different when the scan originates from one's own network. Also, there are high-security sites that do not expect any scans at all. In these cases (and under the corresponding security policies), a scan has to be marked with a high priority.

The alert prioritization step makes use of the information from the impact analysis and the asset database to determine the importance of network services to the overall operation of the network. For each network resource, the asset database contains entries that characterize an asset's security properties. One possible way to perform this characterization is to specify the required levels of *confidentiality*, *integrity*, and *availability* for each asset. The confidentiality property covers the protection of data against its release to unauthorized parties. Availability refers to a resource that is ready to use. The integrity property covers the protection of data against modifications. It is important to note that there is no single value that can capture all security properties of a certain asset. However, different schemes to characterize these properties are possible.

Examples of different levels of security for different assets are given below. A public web service owned by a company may have a low confidentiality value, because the information published through the web service is freely available. However, the integrity and availability values may be high if it is vital for the company to keep the information accurate and available. On the other hand, a mail service might have a high confidentiality value if it is used to exchange confidential e-mail. If the mail system relies on a number of backup mail servers, the availability value for a single server can be low.

The values for the desired security properties are manually entered into the asset database and are not an absolute measure of the importance of any asset, but rather reflect the subjective view of the security administrator. That is, the values depend on the site's security policy and its mission.

In our example scenario, the web service is considered to be important for the operation of the site. Therefore, the meta-alert that summarizes the multistep attack against the Linux machine receives a high priority. All correlated or

Priority	ID	Name	Description	Tag	Reference-Tag
High	12	Meta-Alert	Multistep Attack Scenario		{11, 10}
Low	11	Meta-Alert	Remote Attack Session	correlated	{9, 5}
Low	9	Meta-Alert	Remote Attack Thread	correlated	{8, 4}
Low	8	Meta-Alert	Fused Portscan	correlated	{2, 3}
Low	2	Portscan		correlated	
Low	3	Portscan		correlated	
Low	4	Apache Exploit		correlated	
Low	5	Bad Request		correlated	
Low	10	Meta-Alert	Local Attack Thread	correlated	{6, 7}
Low	6	Local Exploit		correlated	
Low	7	Local Exploit		correlated	
Low	1	IIS Exploit		irrelevant	

Table 6.2. Correlated Output with Priorities for Example Attack Scenario

failed attacks are, as a default action, assigned a low priority. The final output for the example scenario is shown in Table 6.2. As desired, only a single, high-priority alert is presented to the administrator. This meta-alert summarizes the complete attack scenario and combines all alerts that are related to this attack. The remaining alerts are intermediate alerts that are either part of the attack scenario or indications of irrelevant intrusion attempts.

4.   Alert Sanitization

Alert correlation necessitates that alerts from different locations are related (correlated) to obtain insight that cannot be inferred from data at a single location. So far, we have not considered organizational or legal requirements that this process has to meet. In particular, we have not discussed the problem of correlating information from locations that are controlled by different entities. In this case, it might not be desirable (or acceptable under some security policy) for a certain party to make all collected information available to others. This is especially true when the collected data contains sensitive or confidential information.

When multiple parties collaborate and share alert data to perform correlation, there are two conflicting goals. On one hand, the alert data should contain as much detail as possible to support the correlation process. On the other hand, the data should contain as little information as possible to prevent the accidental leaking of confidential or sensitive information. A compromise has to be found that retains as much information as possible while making sure that the data can be shared without disclosing confidential information.

The process of removing or disguising sensitive information from data is called *sanitization*. There are two forms of sanitization, *anonymizing* and *pseudonymizing* sanitization [Flegel, 2002; Pang and Paxson, 2003]. Anonymizing sanitization prevents anyone from reconstructing the original data, while pseudonymizing sanitization can be undone, that is, the original data can be reconstructed. In general, it is desirable to implement pseudonymizing sanitization because this allows access to the original information in case further analysis is required. Consider, for example, the case where an organization forwards sanitized data to a collaborating party that detects an attack in this data. To identify the originator of the attack, the sanitization process needs to be undone. When a pseudonymizing process is used, the organization can recover the original data and identify the attacker.

The key objective of sanitization is to preserve the properties needed for security analysis. These properties are not static but depend on the used analysis techniques. When the analysis changes, new properties might need to be added. This usually requires a resanitization of data to accommodate for the changes, which requires that pseudonymizing techniques be used.

The sanitization process should, besides preserving the properties required for analysis, also satisfy the following requirements [Pang and Paxson, 2003].

- **Understand structure of data.** Sanitizing transformations should understand the structure of the data and only operate on typed values with a clearly defined semantics. Instead of performing transformations on a flat bytestream (e.g., IP packet), a data element should be parsed into fields with an understood meaning (e.g., IP packet header with source and destination IP address). This allows one to focus on potentially sensitive fields and to specify sanitizing operations more precisely.

- **Preserve data integrity.** When a sanitizing transformation is applied to a field, the result should be a syntactically correct data element. This means that the new value that is used to replace the original field has to follow the syntactic rules associated with the field type. In addition, it is also be possible that there are fields that need to be adjusted. Consider, for example, length fields that denote the length of the complete data element or checksums that cover the field that is replaced. In particular, it is complicated to maintain the correct format when a network packet trace is sanitized. When the lengths of TCP packets are changed, it is necessary to update the packet length, and as a result the checksum of the encapsulating IP packet. In addition, the TCP sequence numbers need to be adjusted. When the payload of the packet exceeds the maximum length of an IP packet, additional IP packets need to be introduced to preserve the integrity of the trace.

- **Operate fail-safe.** Fail-safe in the context of sanitization means that only those fields are kept in the resulting data element that have been explicitly marked as non-sensitive or for which a sanitization routine is provided. This requirement mandates the use of "whitelists" that mark fields as acceptable for sharing. This makes it much harder to accidentally include sensitive information in the output.

The information that the sanitization process removes falls into two categories: *identities* such as user and host identifiers, and *attributes* such as passwords or keys. An important first step in the sanitization process is to identify which identities and attributes are present in the data, and which of these need to be removed (recall the desired fail-safe requirement mentioned previously). The next step is to decide how fields of a data element should be sanitized. The following enumeration describes common techniques, again according to [Pang and Paxson, 2003].

- **Constant Substitution.** A straightforward way to sanitize data is to replace each sensitive field with a constant string. Constant substitution can be applied to attributes such as user credentials or keys, but is usually undesirable for identifiers. The reason is that it is no longer possible to distinguish between different identities. In order to keep distinguishable identifiers for identities, a 1-1 mapping approach has to be applied.

- **Sequential Numbering.** Sequential numbering extends constant substitution by appending a sequence number to the constant string. Each distinct identity is consistently marked with a unique number. A drawback of this scheme is the necessity to keep the complete mapping history in order to provide a consistent labeling during the sanitization process. When the labeling need to be consistent among multiple sanitization processes, the mapping history can grow very large.

- **Hashing.** The problem of a mapping history can be solved by replacing the sequential numbering with a hash function. This requires no state during the sanitization. To provide confidentiality, the hash function has to be one way and should be resistant to chosen plaintext attacks. An example for such a hash function is MD5 with a secret key. Assuming that MD5 cannot be reversed and the secret key cannot be obtained, hashing provides a level of confidentiality that is equivalent to sequential numbering.

- **Prefix-preserving Mapping.** All three sanitization techniques presented so far completely alter the structure of the data field they operate on. Sometimes, however, it might be desirable to preserve some of the structural similarities between identities or attributes. An important class of identities that benefit from the preservation of structural similarities are IP addresses. In this case, it might be useful to ensure that any two IP addresses in the original data that share a prefix of k bits will also share a k-bit prefix after sanitization [Xu et al., 2002]. Another example where prefix preservation might be important are directory components of file names. Several techniques have been presented that can provide this kind of sanitization. On the downside, these schemes are also more vulnerable to attacks that the other techniques.

The sanitization techniques mentioned above eliminate direct exposure of confidential identities and attributes. However, other fields, which are not confidential, could be used by an attacker to *indirectly* infer sensitive information. The following provides an overview of common inference techniques.

- **Fingerprinting.** Fingerprinting refers to an attacker that can recover the identity of an object by comparing attributes, which are not removed by the sanitization process, to the attributes of objects with known identities. This technique is only possible when the attacker has knowledge of some objects and their non-sensitive attributes. Common examples of fingerprinting include inferring the name of a file by checking for its length. In other cases, peculiar behavior patterns or timing information can be used to infer sanitized identities.

- **Structure Recognition.** This technique is related to fingerprinting and attempts to reveal the identity of an object by analyzing structural similarities between objects. Consider the case of a network traffic trace where the source and the destination IP addresses are replaced by sequential numbers or hashes. By assuming that such a trace contains scans, an attacker can check for a certain source that connects to a series of different destinations. When it is further assumed that the scan is done sequentially, the order of occurrence of scan targets provides an enumeration of hosts in the target network.

- **Shared-Text Matching.** In the case of hashing, when two identifiers or two attributes share the same text, the unmasking of one element will also reveal the other element. This can be solved by appending the field name to the value before hashing, thus mapping identical field values to different hashes.

- **Known-Text Matching.** When both the original text and the hashed value are known, an attacker can check for all occurrences of the hash value and substitute it with the corresponding original text. This might occur when the attacker is able of inserting chosen plaintext into the audit data before it is sanitized. After sanitization, the attacker can read out the hash value for the previously inserted text.

In current sanitization approaches, a lot of manual effort is required to identify confidential fields and to implement appropriate sanitization routines. So far, there are no general solutions that can (i) completely formalize security considerations, and (ii) automate the process of generating appropriate sanitization schemes. Therefore, it is not possible to automatically *validate* that a sanitization process removes all confidential data.

A formalized sanitization process that can be validated requires a complete view of the threats that the system is exposed to. In addition, a rigorous description of the sanitization techniques is necessary. The sanitization process also needs an understanding of the semantics of the involved data elements.

However, the benefits of automated sanitization would be substantial. Because no or only minimal human effort is required to release sanitized data, many sites could make their network and system log data available to the public. In addition, users that are interested in retaining certain properties in the data could provide their own sanitization routines. When these routines respect the security requirements of the data provider, the results can be forwarded to the user. This process could be handled completely automatically.

Chapter 7

LARGE-SCALE CORRELATION

Alert correlation systems typically collect and correlate audit data that is produced at different, distributed nodes in a network. This is necessary to detect certain attacks that would remain unnoticed by only focusing on local activity.

The alert correlation process that was introduced in the previous chapters is based on a centralized design where all alerts are forwarded to a central location (see Figure 7.1), where they can be further analyzed.

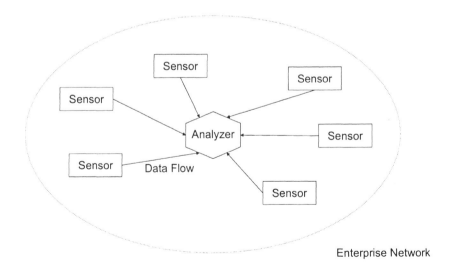

Figure 7.1. Centralized Correlation Schema

However, this design might experience scalability problems when deployed in large network installations. While current approaches work reasonable well for mid-sized networks, large installations with several thousand hosts push them to and above their limits. As networks and traffic grow, the central correlation system can become a performance bottleneck. As a first solution, data reduction schemes have been introduced that forward only relevant parts of the audit stream (and in addition, this data can be compressed).

DIDS [Snapp et al., 1991] was among the first systems that collected data from multiple, distributed sensors at a central location. The two main threat scenarios that DIDS has been designed to handle are so-called *doorknob attacks* and *network browsing*. In a doorknob attack, the intruder's goal is to discover and gain access to insufficiently protected hosts. This is done by trying a few common account and password combinations on each of a number of computers. As the attacker only performs a few logins on each machine, usually using different account names, the sensor on each host might not flag the attack. Network browsing occurs when a user is looking through a number of files on many different computers within a short period of time. The browsing activity level on any single host may not be sufficiently high to raise any alarm by itself.

Because events that are generated by doorknob or network browsing attacks are all independent of each other (and potentially suspicious by themselves), a large amount of low-level filtering and some analysis can already be performed by each host-based monitor. This enables the system to minimize the amount of data that is transferred to the central correlator. However, when events are only suspicious in the context of other events that occur somewhere else, a local data reduction scheme does not work anymore. In that case, all events are potentially relevant and need to be transmitted to the correlator.

Although prefiltering at the local sensors can make the data stream that needs to be transferred to a central analyzer manageable, it is often impossible to decide locally whether information is relevant for the detection of an attack or not. Systems that use local preprocessing can either forward all possible interesting data or take the risk of dropping needed events. In the first case, the original problem is still unsolved, in the latter, the system can miss attacks, which is clearly undesirable. In general, a data reduction scheme that is capable of forwarding only the relevant data for arbitrary threat scenarios is very difficult to realize.

To address these issues, hierarchical variants were developed [Crosbie and Spafford, 1995; Staniford et al., 1996; Porras and Neumann, 1997; Balasubramaniyan et al., 1998], which distribute the computational load and the network traffic over a number of intermediate analyzers. These analyzers attempt to perform detection for a small domain of the whole network and send all reports that might indicate attacks against the whole installation to a master correlation node (as shown in Figure 7.2). This master node then correlates all cross-domain incidents to gain a complete picture of the security posture of the network.

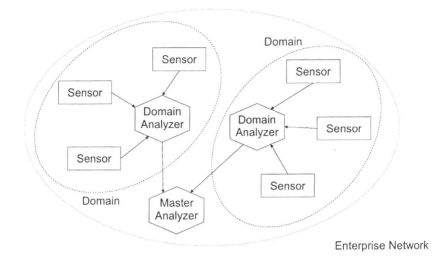

Figure 7.2. Hierarchical Correlation Schema

GrIDS (GRaph-based Intrusion Detection System for large networks) [Staniford et al., 1996] is a hierarchical IDS that has been built in particular to detect distributed attacks against large networks (i.e., distributed scans and worms). Instead of forwarding all audit data to a central location, GrIDS constructs activity graphs. These activity graphs capture network traffic between hosts. Thus, a node in the activity graph represents a single host or, alternatively, a set of aggregated machines and the edges represent network traffic between these nodes.

Activity graphs are constructed using rule sets. That is, given an existing activity graph and a new connection between hosts, rules determine if, and how, this new connection is incorporated into the graph. It is also possible to combine different subgraphs into a new activity graph. Detection is based on graph patterns that are evaluated every time a new graph is constructed.

GrIDS introduces a scalable aggregation mechanism by using different analysis components that only monitor parts of the graph. By reducing the signature of an attack scenario to a graph pattern, a simple and elegant aggregation mechanism is achieved. However, only attacks that manifest themselves as connection graphs (such as worms and denial of service attacks) can be identified.

A more recent hierarchical system is Emerald (Event Monitoring Enabling Responses to Anomalous Live Disturbances) [Porras and Neumann, 1997; Neumann and Porras, 1999], an IDS that combines anomaly-based and misuse-based detection mechanisms and focuses on providing a system for large-scale enterprise networks. Emerald uses a hierarchically layered approach to network surveillance consisting of three tiers. The lowest level, which relies on service analysis monitors, covers the misuse of individual components and network services within the boundary of a single domain. The medium layer, which relies on domain monitors, covers misuse across multiple services and components. The highest layer coordinates activities across multiple domains using enterprise monitors. Enterprise monitors correlate events received from domain monitors and focus on network-wide threats such as spreading worms or large-scale network scans.

Information exchange between monitors is implemented using a publish-subscribe-based communication scheme which allows messages to be sent via a push or pull data exchange. According to [Neumann and Porras, 1999], a significant amount of software engineering effort has been invested into the system to keep it as modularized as possible. The layered, hierarchical approach allows coordinated detection and communication between components. The creators claim to have obtained very promising results with the system. Unfortunately, little details have been provided about the implementation of the publish-subscribe infrastructure used for large-scale correlation. A publish-subscribe approach [Carzaniga et al., 2000] usually requires a communication backbone that is responsible for managing subscriptions and message routing. As both publishers and subscribers change very frequently, this backbone might become a bottleneck and is vulnerable to direct attacks (for example, denial of service that prevents the forwarding of messages).

Hierarchical designs try to distribute alert correlation by using dedicated intermediate nodes that receive all relevant data for a small and manageable area. Only data which is considered to be important for the whole protection domain is forwarded to a central node which is responsible for detecting attacks that affect the whole installation. Although this approach moves the prefiltering decisions to a higher level, the basic shortcoming is still present. While each area is completely monitored by an intrusion detection system, the global correlation process is either overloaded or cut off from relevant data.

Also, both centralized and hierarchical solutions that were discussed so far do not address deliberate attacks against the intrusion detection system itself. When the central node or important intermediate nodes fail, the system is effectively blinded. This is also true for publish-subscribe variants as implemented in Emerald. The reason is that the message routing hosts that manage subscriptions and set up the paths for published messages can be attacked.

In order to solve the fundamental problems of centralized or hierarchical data gathering and dedicated processing nodes, it is necessary to use decentralized data analysis techniques. Although it is difficult to identify independent events and analyze them in parallel, a distributed detection algorithm might still be feasible and beneficial.

A number of different techniques could be used. One approach suggests that only the nodes where the intrusion is actually witnessed cooperate on its detection. Another approach is based on mobile code where agents roam the network and carry the relevant data with them. Finally, a completely decentralized approach could use a peer-to-peer cooperation scheme. The potential advantage of these approaches is scalability, because by using decentralizing analysis it is possible to keep the total amount of traffic between all involved machines as well as the peak load at any single spot manageable.

The Cooperating Security Manager (CSM) approach [White et al., 1996] was the first correlation system to explicitly work without a dedicated node. Instead, independent uniform working entities are installed at each host (called security managers). In order to be able to detect distributed attacks, the different monitors have to coordinate their intrusion detection activities and cooperate (hence the name of the system) as described below.

Each security manager is connected to local intrusion detection sensors. Whenever a local sensor detects a malicious event, it is forwarded to the security manager and the detection process is started. This detection process is based on the tracking of individual users and the notion of a *trail*. A trail is a data structure that stores the information on which host a user originally performed her login and how she continued to connect to different machines from there. Upon the notification of an alert, a security manager sends the alert information to its upstream neighbor (along the trail of the user who is responsible for the alert). The alert follows the trail until it reaches the security manager where the user has initially logged in. Along the trail, all suspicious activities are aggregated and an alarm is raised when too many of those operations have occurred. This happens at the final host of a trail. It is assumed that a user with a longer trail will have done more sensitive actions so the length of the trail is considered when calculating the suspicion level. The design assumes that although a skilled intruder will perform only a small amount of malicious activities on each host, in summary there will be many. By using the trail data, an overall suspicion level for each user can be determined.

The presented fully distributed architecture has the advantage that no single point of failure or bottlenecks are inherent in its design. CSM is intended to scale well and can be used in larger environments. One problem is the fact that only activities of a single user are correlated. When a number of different accounts are compromised, cooperating attackers might remain undetected. Additionally, only threat scenarios that require a user to be logged in and attack the network from inside can be covered. Intrusions from outside targeting inside network services will remain unnoticed.

Sparta [Kruegel et al., 2001] (Security Policy Adaptation Reinforced Through Agents) and Micael [de Queiroz et al., 1999] suggest an approach for intrusion detection with distributed, decision-making agents. In both systems, autonomous agents investigate possible intrusions and are capable of initiating countermeasures against attackers. The idea is that autonomous agents can be "sent" to hosts that are under attack. The agents then continue to gather additional data as required. The main idea is that data does not have to be transfered to a predetermined node; instead agents are moved to the location where the data is already available.

The problem is that mobile code is unnecessary and counterproductive for the given tasks. The agents are solely used as data containers, a task that can be fulfilled more efficiently by sending the information encapsulated in messages. These messages are exchanged between processing modules that are deployed at all nodes in advance. In addition, mobile agents introduce new security risks and cause a performance penalty without providing any clear advantages.

The following sections describe a completely decentralized approach where the detection of an intrusion is restricted to those nodes where parts of the attack are directly observable. The design is related to the Cooperating Security Managers system in the way that it distinguishes between a local intrusion detection component and an information forwarding unit at each node. However, different from CSM, the information exchange between nodes is not limited to the login chain of users. We describe an algorithm that is capable of detecting patterns of alerts that occur at multiple nodes of a network in a completely decentralized fashion. In addition, the specification language to define distributed patterns is explained.

As in the discussion about the correlation process, an intrusion is defined as a pattern of basic alerts that can occur at multiple hosts. The decentralized pattern detection algorithm finds distributed alert patterns by sending messages between nodes where alerts occur. Therefore, each node of the protected network has to run a process that executes the distributed pattern detection algorithm. The detailed description of the layout of such patterns as well as the detection algorithm forms the core of the remaining chapter. By avoiding dedicated central components and by designing a fully distributed system, it is possible to achieve favorable scalability and fault tolerance properties. When a single node in the system fails (or is compromised), it stops its local detection and ceases to forward information. This prevents the detection of pattern instances when attacks occur at the compromised host, however, the rest of the system remains intact. In addition, messages are not sent to designated nodes but are exchanged between equal peers. This helps to distribute the complete message traffic over the network without introducing centralized components that might become performance bottlenecks.

A potential drawback of a completely distributed design is the possibly large amount of messages that are exchanged between nodes. This potential danger is addressed in the following sections.

1. Pattern Specification

The design of the pattern specification language is guided by two conflicting goals. The first one demands a language that should be as expressive as possible. It would be desirable to allow the description of complex relationships between attacks on different hosts using regular or tree grammars. As the system relies on peer-to-peer message passing between hosts without a central coordination point, arbitrarily complex patterns might cause an explosion in the amount of data that needs to be exchanged. In the worst case, each node has to send all its data to every other node. This conflicts with the second goal, which demands that the amount of data that has to be transferred between hosts should be as small as possible. Therefore, one has to impose limitations on the expressiveness of the pattern language.

1.1 Definitions

A pattern describes activities on individual hosts as well as interactions between machines. The basic building block of a pattern is a sequence of alerts that happens locally on one machine (called *host sequence*). One can specify a list of alerts at a local host by enumerating them and imposing certain constraints on their attributes. A distinction is made between constraints that relate single alert attributes with constant values and constraints that relate different attributes of alerts using variables. One can use the standard logical operators for both types of constraints and an extended set of operators (including in and range) to relate attributes with constants. A connection (context) between alerts sequences on different hosts is established by *send events*.

Definition:

> *A pattern* P, *relating alerts that occur at n distinct hosts, consists of n sequences of alerts, one for each node (an alert sequence at a single node is called a host sequence).*
>
> *A set of alerts* S_A *at host* A *is linked to a set of alerts* S_B *at host* B, *if* S_A *contains a send event to host* S_B. *Any event that refers to a remote host (e.g. the sending of a packet to a host, the reception of a packet from a host) might be used as a send event.*

It is only required for a send event that its target B can be determined locally at S_A from the event data.

Consider the case of a portscan that attempts to identify active HTTP ports on the hosts of a target network. When the firewall detects such a scan **and** knows the address of the network's web server, the occurrence of that portscan can be utilized as a send event. In this case, the target host (i.e., the web server) is locally known to the node that identifies the suspicious behavior. Therefore, the firewall has all information available to inform the web server.

The first alert of S_B has to be the next alert to occur after the send event in S_A. It is required that the send event be the last event in S_A.

Definition:

Pattern P *is valid, if the following properties hold.*

1 Each set of alerts is at least linked to one other set.

2 Every set except one (called the root set) contains exactly one send event as the last event of the host sequence. The root set contains no send event.

3 The connection graph contains no cycles. The connection graph is built by considering each alert set as a vertex and each link between two sets as an edge between the corresponding vertices.

These definitions allow only tree-like pattern structures (i.e., the connection graph is a tree), where the node with the root set is the root of the tree. Although this restriction seems limiting at first glance, most interesting situations can be described. Usually, activity at a target host depends on activity that has occurred earlier at several other hosts. This situation can be easily described by the tree patterns where connection links from those hosts end at the root set.

The case where activity on two different nodes both depend on the occurrence of a single event at a third node cannot be directly expressed in the pattern language (as there would be two root sets). Nevertheless, a centralized application might split the original, illegal pattern into subpatterns (each representing a legal tree-like structure) and relate the results itself.

1.2   Attack Specification Language

This section describes the syntax and semantics of the pattern description language, which is called **Attack Specification Language (ASL)**. A pattern definition is written as follows

```
'ATTACK' "Scenario Name" '[' nodes ']' pattern
```

The *nodes* section is used to assign an identifier to each node that is later referred to in the pattern definition.

The *pattern* section specifies the pattern itself. It consists of a list of alert sets, one for each node that appears in the node section. The alert set, which represents the host sequence, is a list of identifiers, each describing an alert. A predefined label called send is used to identify the target node of send events.

Each alert can optionally be defined more precisely by constraints on the alert's attribute values. These attribute values can be related to constant values or to variables by a number of operators (=, !=, <, >, >= and <=). In addition, attribute values can be related to constant values by a range or an in operator. The argument of range is a pair of values specifying the upper and lower bound of a valid range of values, while the argument of in is a list that enumerates all possible values. More formally, these operators are defined below.

$$x \text{ range } (x_0, x_1) \leftrightarrow x_0 \leq x \leq x_1$$
$$x \text{ in } (x_0, x_1, ..., x_n) \leftrightarrow \exists i \, (0 \leq i \leq n) \text{ and } x = x_i$$

A variable is defined the first time it is used. One must assign a value (bind an attribute value) to each defined variable exactly once, while the variable may be used arbitrarily often as a right argument in constraint definitions. The scope of variables is global and its type is inherited from the defining attribute.

For each alert, an optional response function can be specified. This function is invoked whenever the corresponding alert description is fulfilled and it can take the values of already bound variables, alert attributes, or constants as arguments. A response function can be used to generate alerts for the system administrator or to perform active countermeasures against an intruder (e.g., the reconfiguration of firewall rules).

In addition, response functions can be used to create *artificial alert objects* that are fed back into the detection process. An artificial alert is not related to an actual activity in the environment, but is created during a response by the system itself. It is fed back into the local node's input queue and can be utilized to satisfy constraints of different patterns. Artificial alerts are a useful mechanism to exchange information between attack scenarios or to model timeouts. The output of a certain attack pattern can be used as input for another pattern to build hierarchical structures or to implement scenarios that count the number of times a certain basic pattern has occurred. A timeout can be implemented by starting a timer in a response function that then creates an artificial alert when it expires.

1.3   Language Grammar

With these explanations, the syntax of the pattern section can be specified in BNF as follows.

```
pattern     : {alert set}+
alert set   : node-id '{' {alert}+ '}'
alert       : ['send('target-id'):'] alert-id '[' {constraint ';' }* ']'
constraint  : assignment | [label] relation [response]
assignment  : '$'variable-id '=' ( attribute | constant )
relation    : attribute operator ['('] {value ',' }* value [')']
value       : constant | '$'variable-id
attribute   : alert-attr-id
operator    : '='|'!='|'<'|'>'|'>='|'<='| 'in'|'range'
response    : '<' function-id'(' arg-list ')' '>'
arg-list    : { arg-id ',' }* arg-id | e
*-id        : string
constant    : string | number
```

The following example shows a classic distributed scenario, namely an island-hop scenario. In this attack an intruder tries to hide her tracks by performing a number of consecutive logins into different machines. All log files except one (the host where the attacker first compromised the network's security perimeter) show only connections from trusted machines. Different local time settings and audit file policies often make it difficult to trace back such a chain of logins. Although the scenario itself does not describe an actual attack, such behavior is still suspicious enough to alert an administrator.

```
ATTACK "Island-Hop" [ Node1, Node2 ]
Node1 {
  send(Node2): tcp_connect [ DstPort == 22; ]
}
Node2 {
  tcp_connect [ DstPort == 22; ] < alert(DstIP); >
}
```

The scenario above describes a ssh connection from Node1 to port 22 at Node2, and from there to port 22 of a third remote machine. Node2 is the root set (i.e., the node with no outgoing send events). The target of the send event at Node1 can easily be extracted as the destination IP address of the tcp_connect event attribute. The IP address of that host (specified as the DstIP attribute) can be extracted at Node2 and is passed as an argument to the response function alert which notifies the administrator.

2.   Pattern Detection

The purpose of the pattern detection process is to identify alert instances that satisfy an attack scenario written in ASL. When a set of alerts fulfills the temporal and content constraints of a scenario, an alarm can be raised. Notice that instead of simply sending a message to a central system administration console (that yields again a single point of failure), more sophisticated responses can be implemented. The node itself can issue commands to reconfigure a firewall or to terminate offending network connections, thereby eliminating the single point of failure introduced by the central console of a human operator.

2.1   Basic Data Structures

In order to be able to process an attack description, it has to be translated from ASL into data structures suitable for the detection process.

Pattern Graph

This is done by transforming a scenario into a directed, acyclic graph, which is called *pattern graph*. An attack scenario describes sequences of alerts located at different hosts that are connected by send events. Each single alert specified by an ASL scenario is represented as a node of the resulting graph. The nodes of each host sequence are connected by directed edges. An edge leads from a node representing a certain alert to the node which represents the immediate successor of that event in the ASL pattern description. Send events require a different treatment as they are the last event in their host sequence and therefore do not have an immediate successor. In this case, a directed edge leads to the first node of the host sequence pointed to by the send event.

The resulting graph shows a tree shape and all paths through the graph end at the last event of the root set's sequence (called *root node*). Each node receives a unique identification number that consists of a part that identifies the attack scenario itself and a part that identifies each node within the scenario. The following example (see Figure 7.3) shows the result of such a transformation, which is straightforward as ASL only allows tree-shaped patterns. The attack scenario describes a pattern of a potential attack against a web server by a variant of the *Code Red* worm. Similar to the intruder described in the introduction in Section 1, this virus does not only scan for an open port 80 but also attempts to retrieve the type of operating system the web server runs on by asking the DNS server for the web server's HINFO (hardware and OS info) entry. This allows the virus to target Microsoft IIS servers more accurately. In this scenario, an alarm is raised whenever a portscan detector notices a scan against port 80 from a certain IP address, and the DNS server gets HINFO queries from the same address, and finally the web server receives an HTTP request from that source.

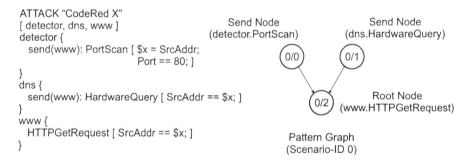

Figure 7.3. Pattern Graph Transformation

Messages

The detection algorithm does not deal with alerts itself, instead, it operates on messages. A message is a compact, more suitable representation of an alert. Most attack descriptions rely only on a small subset of the alert's attributes for correlation (e.g., only IP addresses instead of the complete IP header information). In ASL, only attributes that are assigned or compared to variables are of interest to the detection process. Therefore, there is no need to operate on complete alert objects.

Obviously, a single alert can match the description of several attack scenario patterns. Thus, if more than one description is matched, several message instances (one for each matching pattern) are created. Whenever a message is created, all relevant attributes (i.e., the attributes that are assigned or compared to variables in the ASL description) are copied into it. Then, the message is forwarded to the node representing the matching alert description for further processing.

Each message can be written as a triple <ID, timestamp, list of (attribute, value)>. The *ID* of the message is set to the identification of the node of the pattern graph. The *timestamp* denotes the time of occurrence of the original event and the *attribute/value* list holds the values of the relevant event attributes that have been taken from the original event attributes. The ID of a message defines its type. Different actual message instances with an identical ID are considered to be of the same message type.

It is possible that messages of different types receive different attributes from a single event - depending on which ones are actually used in the attack description. In addition, the attribute/value list can be empty when the corresponding ASL event pattern does not reference any variables at all. In Figure 7.3, a portscan event that targets port 80 from IP address 128.131.0.1 would cause the creation of the message of type 0/0 with the format <0/0, time of occurrence, (SrcAddr, 128.131.0.1)>.

2.2 Constraints

An attack description in ASL imposes a number of different constraints on the events that must be taken into account by the detection algorithm. The set of constraints can be divided into *temporal*, *static*, and *dynamic* subsets.

Temporal Constraints

The paths through the pattern graph reflect the temporal relationships between alerts. Alert A has to occur before alert B if and only if B is on the path which leads from A to the root node. The alerts of a host sequence have to occur in the same order as they are defined in the ASL description. When a host sequence is linked to another host sequence by a send event, all alerts of the destination sequence have to occur after the send event in the source sequence.

Static Constraints

An alert pattern that relates an alert attribute to a constant value imposes a static constraint onto alerts (e.g., the equality relation between the Port attribute and the value 80 in the PortScan event in Figure 7.3). Static constraints are easy to evaluate immediately as soon as a new alert of the appropriate type is received. When an alert satisfies all static constraints of a certain node (respectively, its corresponding alert pattern), a new message instance is created and forwarded to that node. Static constraints are used to decide which messages need to be created from a certain alert, but are not used later during the actual detection process.

Dynamic Constraints

A dynamic constraint is introduced by the use of variables in an attack description. The definition of a variable in an alert pattern and the subsequent use of this variable in other alert patterns introduces relationships between attributes of different alerts.

The definition of a variable by a certain alert attribute and its subsequent use as an operand in a relation with another attribute creates a direct relation between these two attributes. In Figure 7.3 above, the definition of variable x as the the value of attribute SrcAddr in the PortScan alert description and its use in the equality operations with the attributes of the HardwareQuery and HTTPGetRequest alerts create the following two dynamic constraints.

[PortScan.SrcAddr == HardwareQuery.SrcAddr]
[PortScan.SrcAddr == HTTPGetRequest.SrcAddr]

Attributes that define or that are related to variables are copied into messages. Therefore, it is possible to express the relationship between alert attributes as (dynamic) constraints on the values of their corresponding message types. It cannot always be immediately determined whether an alert satisfies its dynamic constraints, hence alerts that satisfy all static constraints of a certain alert pattern cause a message to be created and passed to the appropriate node (the one which is associated with that alert). It is the task of the actual detection process to resolve all dynamic and temporal constraints.

2.3   Detection Process

The basic detection process can be explained as follows. We have already stated that alerts cause messages to be forwarded to their corresponding nodes more precisely, to the nodes that are associated with matching alerts. The messages may then be moved along the directed edge of the graph to other nodes according to certain rules. The idea is that each node can be considered as the root of a subtree of the complete tree pattern. There are **node constraints** assigned to each node of the graph such that if there are messages which satisfy these node constraints, then there are alerts that fulfill the dynamic and temporal constraints of the complete subtree above that node. Whenever the node constraints of a node are satisfied, certain messages may be moved one step closer to the root node, hence, they are pushed over the node's outgoing edge to its neighbor node below. Because the graph is tree-shaped, there is at most one outgoing edge for each node. Then, these messages are processed at the destination node. This allows the process to successively satisfy subtrees of the complete pattern and move messages closer to the root node of the pattern graph. Whenever messages at the root node fulfill the constraints there, the pattern has been detected (i.e., there exist alerts that satisfies all constraints of the attack scenario).

The advantage of this approach is the fact that only local information in the form of a set of node constraints is necessary to decide which messages should be forwarded. This allows one to distribute nodes of the pattern graph over several hosts and have each node make local decisions without a central coordination point. Different host sequences may potentially occur at different hosts.

Node Constraints

The node constraints have to ensure that all alerts described by the subtree pattern have occurred, that their temporal order is correct, and that all dynamic constraints that can be resolved up to this point are met. The messages that are important for a certain node to satisfy its node constraints belong to one of the following three groups.

- Messages that are created from alerts that match the alert description of the node itself (i.e., that have the same ID as the node). Obviously, in order to satisfy a pattern, one alert for each node of that pattern is needed. To fulfill a subpattern originating at a node, it is necessary to receive at least one message created from an alert that matches the local event description itself (such a message is called a *local message* for that node).

- Messages that are created from events that match the event description of the node's immediate predecessors in the pattern graph. Usually each node has only one predecessor but this number can vary for the first node of each host sequence. Such nodes may have more than one predecessor or none at all.

- Messages whose value(s) are used in at least one dynamic constraint at that node.

The node constraints consist of

1 the set of temporal constraints between the local message and the predecessor nodes' local messages **and**

2 all dynamic constraints that can be resolved at this node.

The set of the temporal constraints between the local message and its predecessor messages guarantees that alerts described by the local node and by all its immediate predecessors have occurred. As messages from predecessor nodes may only be forwarded by them when the alerts at their predecessor nodes have occurred as well, it is assured that all alerts specified by a subtree pattern have occurred in the correct temporal order. The node constraints have to be modified for nodes without predecessors. For those, it is only necessary that the local message exists.

A dynamic constraint between attributes of two different alerts can be resolved as soon as both operands are available. When messages representing the two alerts are at hand, their relation can be evaluated and one can determine whether the dynamic constraint is satisfied or not. Therefore, every dynamic constraint (i.e., a variable definition at one node and its use at another one) is inserted into the pattern graph at the earliest node possible. The earliest possible node is determined by finding the first common node in the paths from each of the constraint operands to the pattern graph's root node. When one node is on the path of the other one, the constraint is inserted directly there, otherwise it is inserted at the node where both paths merge. A pattern graph with dynamic constraints is shown in Figure 7.4.

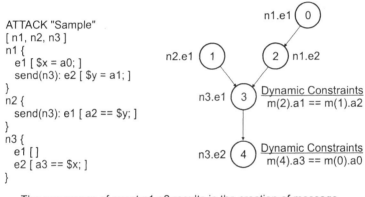

ATTACK "Sample"
[n1, n2, n3]
n1 {
  e1 [$x = a0;]
  send(n3): e2 [$y = a1;]
}
n2 {
  send(n3): e1 [a2 == $y;]
}
n3 {
  e1 [ ]
  e2 [a3 == $x;]
}

The occurrence of event n1.e2 results in the creation of message
<2, time of occurrence, (a1, value of a1)>

Figure 7.4. Complete Pattern Graph

A problem arises when transitive relations are introduced by relating a single message to several other messages. The attributes of alerts that are independent at first glance become linked by being related to a common, third alert. In this case, it is not enough to insert the constraints at the earliest possible node.

Consider the pattern graph in Figure 7.5 and suppose that the following messages:
<0, t1, (a1,0)>, <0, t2, (a1,1)>, <1, t3, (a2,0)>, <1, t4, (a2,1)>, and <3, t5, (a3,0)>
are received in that order. The first four messages (the first two from node 0, the next two from node 1) are eventually passed to node 3 as the value of the first and the third message (which is 0) as well as the value of the second and fourth message (which is 1) are equal (dynamic constraint evaluated at node 2).

As the attributes of messages with ID 1 and 2 are not compared again at node 3, the value of the final (fifth) message is equal to the value of the first message and smaller than the value of the fourth one. This results in an illegal report of a successful match.

To prevent this problem, all dynamic constraints that are connected by having attributes of common messages as their operands are combined in a subset of the scenario constraints called a *cluster*. When a dynamic constraint operates on messages that are used in no other dynamic constraints, the message itself becomes a cluster. In Figure 7.5, all three dynamic constraints are part of a single cluster.

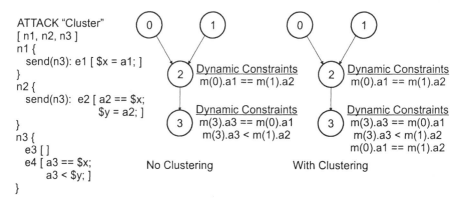

m(x).y indicates the value of attribute y of a message with id x

Figure 7.5.   Constraint Clustering

In addition to the insertion of each constraint at the earliest possible node, all constraints of a cluster are additionally inserted at the cluster root node (but, obviously, no duplicate constraints are inserted). Similar to the situation with a single constraint, the cluster root node is the first common node of all the paths that lead from each operand of every cluster constraint to the root node of the pattern graph. With these additional constraints, the example messages listed above do not result in a false detection.

Message and Bypass Pool

Each node has a *message pool* and a *bypass pool*.x The message pool is a cache that stores message instances that are needed to evaluate the local node constraints. The bypass pool holds message instances that can potentially satisfy node constraints of nodes that are closer to the root of the pattern graph but which are not used for the current node constraints. Messages in the bypass pool are forwarded as soon as their temporal constraints are met.

After the node constraints have been determined, it is easy to calculate the types of the messages for the message pool and the bypass pool. Obviously, the message pool for each node consists of all message types that are used in at least one of its node constraints.

The message types needed for the bypass pools are determined next. For each message type, every node on the path between the first and the last use of messages of that type is examined. When the message type is not contained in the message pool of a node on that path, it is added to the bypass pool there. This assures that messages which are needed to determine node constraints at nodes closer to the root are correctly forwarded there.

The table below shows the node constraints and the types of messages that must be inserted into the message and bypass pools for the pattern graph in Figure 7.4.

Nodes	Node Constraints	Dynamic Constraints	Message / Bypass Pools
0	$\exists m(0)$		$\{m(0)\}$ / $\{\}$
1	$\exists m(1)$		$\{m(1)\}$ / $\{\}$
2	$m(2).t > m(0).t$		$\{m(0), m(2)\}$ / $\{\}$
3	$m(3).t > m(1).t$	$m(2).a1 == m(1).a2$	$\{m(1), m(2), m(3)\}$ /
	$m(3).t > m(2).t$		$\{m(0)\}$
4	$m(4).t > m(3).t$	$m(4).a3 == m(0).a0$	$\{m(0), m(3), m(4)\}$ /
			$\{\}$

Table 7.1. Node Constraints and Message / Bypass Pools

Detection Algorithm

Once the node constraints, the message pool, and the bypass pool have been determined for each node, the algorithm to actually move messages between nodes can be executed. When a new message is received, the ID of the message is checked to determine whether it should go to the message pool or to the bypass pool. When it belongs to neither group, it is simply discarded. This prevents messages from being moved further towards the root node when they are not needed anymore. When the message belongs to the bypass pool, it is put there and no immediate further actions are necessary. Otherwise, it is added to the message pool. Whenever a new message is inserted into the message pool, the node constraints are checked. The algorithm attempts to find a *tuple* of messages of *different* types (i.e., all with distinct identifications) that match *all* the node constraints. The tuple has to include one actual message instance of each message type (i.e., message ID) of the message pool and the new message has to be part of the tuple as well. Consider a potential tuple for node 3 in Figure 7.4, where the message pool is {m1, m2, m3}. The tuple must consist of message instances with the IDs 1, 2 and 3. When such a tuple (or tuples, when more than one set of different messages match the node constraints) can be identified, the detection process has found messages that match the subtree pattern starting at the local node. All of the tuple's messages have to be moved over the outgoing link to the next node. Because messages in the message pool might be needed later to satisfy the node constraints when composed with new messages, the original messages remain in the pool and copies of the messages are forwarded. To prevent the system from being flooded by duplicate messages, each message pool entry is only copied and forwarded to the next node once. For each tuple that matches the local constraints, the bypass pool is inspected. The temporal constraints between each message in the bypass pool and all messages of the matching tuple are checked. When a bypass pool message satisfies all temporal constraints between itself and every tuple message, it is removed from the pool and moved to the next node. This is needed to make sure that only messages which do not violate any temporal constraints are passed on.

The situation is slightly different for send nodes. As a send node can have different next neighbor nodes at different hosts (depending on the target of the send event), the copying of message pool entries and the deletion of bypass pool elements must be handled differently. The send node has to keep track of which message pool entries have already been copied and which bypass pool elements have already been removed and forwarded to the destinations of the send events, for each different destination. This implies that bypass pool elements can never be deleted because they might have to be sent to a completely new destination host. However, elements cannot be kept infinitely long because memory is a limited resource. To address this problem, one can use timers to remove elements from the message and the bypass pools after a certain, configurable time span. This means that patterns which evolve over a long time might remain undetected. Note that this is not a limitation of the approach in particular but a problem that affects all systems that operate online and have to keep state. Such systems need a policy that decides which messages to delete when the available memory is exhausted.

The example in Figure 7.6 shows a step-by-step detection of the distributed pattern which is described by the scenario in Figure 7.4 (also using the node constraints of Figure 7.4). Each tuple of messages that is identified by the correlation process is underlined in the figure. Dotted arrows indicate the copying of messages to the next neighbor. Two sets enclosed in brackets are associated

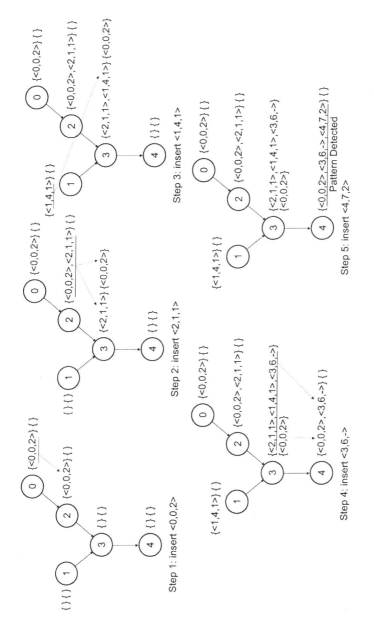

Figure 7.6. Sample Pattern Detection

with each node. The first holds the node's current message pool entries, the second its bypass pool elements.

Discussion

This section briefly discusses the correctness of the detection algorithm. The detection algorithm is correct when it reports an intrusion if and only if alerts occur that satisfy the pattern that the algorithm attempts to detect. A brief informal explanation is given why this is the case.

The explanation is given recursively on the tree shape of the attack scenario pattern. A node only forwards alert information to its (single) successor node in the pattern tree when alerts have occurred that match the pattern subtree above this node (which includes the node itself as the root of that subtree). This implies that all alerts of the subtree have occurred in the correct temporal order and satisfy all dynamic constraints which can be resolved up to this point.

A subtree above a node is satisfied when all local alerts at a node have been detected, the send events of all predecessors have been received, and all dynamic constraints are satisfied. As stated above, the predecessor nodes may only forward messages when the subtrees above those nodes have been satisfied as well. This means that the current node only has to check for the occurrence of the local alerts and must consider all dynamic constraints that can be resolved at that node. More precisely, the algorithm attempts to find the occurrence of local alerts in the correct order that meet all local dynamic constraints. These dynamic constraints have been inserted at the earliest node where they can be resolved.

When the subtree above the root of the pattern is satisfied, alerts that match the whole tree have been found. In this case, the complete scenario is found, and possible countermeasures are executed.

2.4   Implementation Issues

The distributed detection algorithm that is described in the previous section is implemented by correlation components that have to be installed at every host that participates in the cooperative detection process. These components typically receive events from local sensors, and they are responsible for exchanging appropriate messages with collaborating peers. The correlation components are installed on a significant fraction of the hosts in a network and have to process a potentially large amount of messages. Therefore, it is important to efficiently implement the necessary algorithms. This section suggests several improvements over a naive solution.

Whenever the correlation component receives a new event element (either produced by a local sensor or encapsulated in a message), this event has to be forwarded to the appropriate scenarios. Appropriate scenarios are scenarios that refer somewhere in the scenario description to the type of event that has been received. An optimization can be implemented that prevents events of certain types from being forwarded to scenarios when it is impossible that these are part of a pattern, although the type is used in the scenario description. This is the case when a pattern includes local sequences with more than one event (i.e., node sequences of length two or longer). As it is required that all local events occur consecutively, it is not necessary to consider the second (or any later) position in the sequence when the first event has not been seen yet.

This leads to the definition of *active* event types. The set of active event types for an attack scenario only includes event types that can potentially be part of an ongoing intrusion. That means that immediately after system initialization, only the types of the first events of all node sequences in the scenario need to be considered active. As an attack progresses, currently active events are detected. This causes their successor events in the host sequence to be activated as well. It is also possible to deactivate events in the case that a predecessor event in the sequence times out and is removed from the detection process. The active events for each scenario can be stored in an *active events table* which has to be consulted before forwarding events to the relevant scenarios.

The processing of an event by the correlation component is straightforward. The important data structures for the algorithm are already present as they have been calculated offline. After moving the event to all appropriate nodes in the pattern graph, the only difficult part is to determine efficiently the tuples of messages of *different* type that match *all* the node constraints (as explained in the previous section).

To calculate the valid message tuples in a naive way, it is necessary to determine all subsets (derived from the set of messages in the message pool) that contain the newly arrived message and have elements (i.e., messages) of the correct types. Then, it is necessary to check for each subset whether the contained messages satisfy all node constraints and discard those that do not.

Unfortunately, the amount of these subsets is proportional to n^l where n is the number of messages stored at a node and l is the cardinality of the subset. Therefore, it is computationally too expensive to proceed in this manner. The problem can be solved by keeping all message combinations that do not violate any node constraint in a search tree. Instead of storing only the messages themselves and creating new tuples every time a new message arrives, all partially complete tuples that are valid (i.e., that violate no node constraint) are stored. A simple search tree is shown in Figure 7.7. The message pool consists of three different message types with ID 0 (m(0)), ID 1 (m(1)), and ID 2 (m(2)). The "constraints table" lists the the constraints between the attribute values of the messages. Currently, the message pool contains five message instances. All partial tuples that satisfy the constraints have been inserted into the search tree, which is a binary tree with 2^3 leaves (2^l, where l is the number of different message types used for the message pool). A path from the root to a leaf determines the types of messages that are associated with that leaf. Choosing the left child of a node implies that the message type which corresponds to this node is included, choosing the right child implies that the message type is excluded from the partial tuple. The number in each box that is associated with every terminal node shows the number of valid partial tuples that belong to this leaf.

Constraints   Message Pool
m(0).value == m(1).value   m(0): <0, t₁, 1> <0, t₂, 2>
m(0).value < m(2).value   m(1): <1, t₃, 1> <1, t₄, 2>
m(1).value < m(2).value   m(2): <2, t₅, 2>

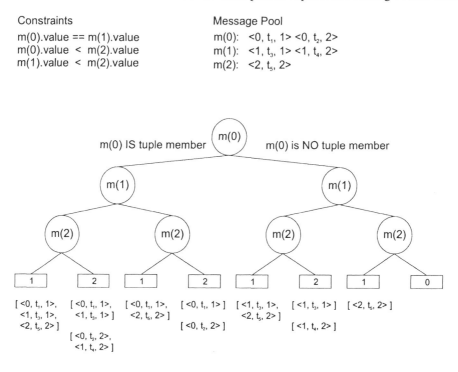

Figure 7.7. Message Tuple Calculation

Whenever a new message arrives, it is added to all partially complete tuples that do not include the type of the new message. When this results in a new partially complete tuple that is still valid, it is simply added to the search tree. When the result is a complete tuple, it is used for further processing. Most of the time, however, a violation of a node constraint is detected and the result is discarded. This approach trades storage space for speed. Instead of checking all message subsets for their validity every time a new message is received, all partially complete tuples that are valid are already stored. Because the total amount of valid tuples is only a very small fraction of the amount of all possible subsets, the size of the tree is manageable. In our experiments, the size of the trees at a single node remained under a few megabytes even in the case of several thousand events. The processing of a new event was handled in a few milliseconds.

Chapter 8

EVALUATION

Since their first introduction, intrusion detection systems have been evaluated using a number of different means. Numerous features of an intrusion detection system can be evaluated. These features ranges from performance and correctness to usability. However, most tests that have been performed have mainly focused on measuring the accuracy and effectiveness of sensors, that is, the false alarm rate and the percentage of attacks that are successfully detected. Little attention have been paid to the other metrics.

1. Evaluation of Traditional ID Sensors

While traditional IDSs could be evaluated using different procedures, one test methodology is predominant. This methodology utilizes synthetically generated audit data that is fed to the sensors under test. The audit data contains a mix of legitimate traffic and attacks. The sensors are evaluated by comparing the true positive rate (i.e., the percentage of attacks that were correctly recognized) and the false positive rate (i.e., the percentage of legitimate traffic flagged as an attack).

Synthetic audit data is usually generated by constructing a testbed network that resembles a real-life organization's network (for instance a military network or a corporate network). On this network, applications and services that are commonly used by the target organization are installed, and user interactions with the applications are simulated using some model of normal user behavior. Examples of simulated user actions include web browsing, e-mail reading and file copying. During the simulation, audit data is collected from the testbed. This audit data usually consists of network traffic sniffed from the network and various log files from the monitored hosts. Attacks are simulated by running prepared attack scripts. Each time an attack script is run, the time and other details about the attack is recorded. The record of all the attacks are usually referred to as the *truth file*. The truth file is used during the scoring to calculate true and false positive rates.

1.1   Evaluation Efforts

Several independent evaluations of IDSs have been performed, most notably the MIT Lincoln Lab evaluations [MIT Lincoln Laboratory, 2000]. These evaluations were a DARPA-sponsored effort to evaluate existing research on intrusion detection. In total, three evaluations were performed in years 1998, 1999, and 2000.

Even though the focus of these evaluations differs slightly for each year, the testing methodology is roughly the same. For the 1998 Lincoln Lab evaluation, a testbed was created to mimic a real-world computer network. Human inter-action with the hosts was simulated using different scripts. The different hosts had different roles, for instance, a secretary computer would be running typi-cal office applications, whereas a developer's host would be running software development tools. Some of the hosts were actual machines, while others were only simulated. Much effort was spent on ensuring that the testbed network looked as real as possible to outside observers.

During the testbed operation, different audit data was collected. All network traffic was collected using tcpdump [tcpdump, 2002]. Also, the hosts syslog files were recorded. In addition, some of the hosts that were running the Solaris operating system had BSM (Basic Security Module) [Sun Microsystems, Inc., 1991] installed. This Basic Security Module, among other things, monitored every system call invocation. Also, every attack was explicitly logged to provide a truth file, which would be used later in the scoring of the IDSs.

For the evaluation, two different data sets were generated. The actual scoring of the IDSs was done offline. The first dataset was provided to the participants along with their corresponding truth file before the actual test. The idea was to give the participants a chance to tune their systems. This dataset was also used to train the anomaly detection systems. The actual evaluation was then performed using the second dataset. The truth file of this dataset was used in the scoring of the sensors and was not disclosed to the participants until after the evaluation had ended. The result of the Lincoln Lab 1998 evaluation was a measure of each sensor's true positive and false positive rates.

Lincoln Lab performed a similar evaluation in 1999. The test setup was roughly the same as in the previous year. However, the differences were that the performed attacks were stealthier and that participants were given attack-free training data instead of training data with labeled attacks. The reason for giving the participants attack-free data was that most anomaly systems require this type of data in order to train their sensors.

1.2   Problems

Several people have criticized the Lincoln Lab datasets, with the best known critique presented in [McHugh, 2000]. The general opinion is that the models used to generate background traffic were too simple, and if real background traffic was used, the false positive rate would be much higher. Another problem was that, in some cases, the attack traffic had features that made it easily distinguishable from legitimate traffic. For instance, in the 1998 dataset, the time-to-live (TTL) value of the IP packets belonging to attacks was different from the TTL value of background traffic packets.

To make up for some of the shortcomings of artificially created audit data, people have tried using real audit data from production networks for IDS testing purposes. Unfortunately, this approach has two major drawbacks. First, no truth file can be created for data collected from a production system. If the system is connected to the Internet, then anyone can attack the system at any time. It would be difficult (if not impossible) to identify all audit records caused by malicious activity. The second problem with using real world data is that the rate of successful compromises in a production system is very low. A system must potentially be monitored for a long period of time before a successful attack is seen.

An approach that combines the advantages of real-world traffic and synthetic datasets is the use of honeypots. A honeypot is a host (or, in some cases, a whole network) that is deliberately configured to contain vulnerable services. It is then connected to the Internet, the idea being that attackers who scan large IP blocks looking for vulnerable hosts would eventually find the honeypot and break into it. This solves some of the problems that occur when using production network traffic. Since the honeypot is not used for any legitimate purpose, all activity on the honeypot is considered intrusive, and there is no need to create a truth file. Also, the rate of successful compromise in a honeypot is potentially much higher than in a production system, since the honeypot has several vulnerable services installed. A problem with honeypots is the total lack of legitimate background traffic. Also, if the honeypot is not located close to a real production system, it might not attract attackers who target only specific networks which they believe contain valuable assets (as opposed to attackers who randomly scan IP blocks). In general, more focused attackers are believed to be more skillful, and their attacks are potentially more interesting than the more common "script kiddie" behavior.

2.   Evaluation of Alert Correlators

For an IDS sensor, the detection rate (i.e., true positive rate) and the false positive rate are good measures of its effectiveness. However, for an alert correlation system, these values often cannot easily be calculated.

On problem is that for a correlator, a false positive is not clearly defined. A correlator operates on the output of IDS sensors and it receives an input alert only when one of the low-level sensors reports an attack. If this input event is a false positive, and the correlator (falsely) draws a conclusion that an attack is ongoing, one might argue that this is the fault of the low-level sensor and that not of the correlator. Thus, the correlator should not be penalized for drawing such a conclusion unless the correlator somehow could have validated that the input alert was a false positive, for example, by using one of the validation techniques presented earlier in this book.

Another problem is the calculation of the detection rate. It is possible that an attack is only creating a single low-level alert. For instance, if a buffer overflow vulnerability of a service is exploited over an encrypted network connection, any network-based IDS would not be able to detect this intrusion. The only IDS that has access to the unencrypted data and might be able to detect the intrusion is a host-based IDS running on the victim machine. This IDS might only emit one alert in response to the attack and a correlator receiving this alert should not correlate this with any other alert, as this attack is only represented by a single alert (assuming that the attacker did not perform any scanning prior to the attack and no actions that were detected afterwards). Since no correlation can be performed, the correlator should not output any report in response to the input alert. However, this should not be considered a missed attack and should not cause a reduction in the detection rate.

2.1   Evaluation Efforts

Lincoln Lab 2000

The success of the previous Lincoln Lab evaluation efforts motivated the MIT Lincoln Laboratory group to generate new datasets in 2000. Because of the growing interest in evaluating techniques for the detection of complex attacks, these datasets were geared towards multistep attack scenarios. The testbed network in this evaluation was more complex than in the previous evaluations: A firewall protected the testbed from the (simulated) Internet. The attacker was located on the outside of this firewall and was performing more realistic attack scenarios. On of these scenarios represented an intrusion where an outsider scanned all hosts to identify all reachable hosts. This scanning phase was followed by a more detailed scan of the hosts that had been found reachable in the previous phase. Hosts that were found to be vulnerable to a particular sadmind[1] exploit were broken into and a DDoS tool was installed on the target computers. Finally, the attacker initiated a DDoS attack against an off-site network using the previously compromised hosts.

---

[1] sadmind is a Solaris service used for remote administration of hosts

Cyber Panel Correlation Validation Effort

As the focus of many researchers shifted from low-level attack detection to high-level attack analysis and intent recognition, it was necessary to devise new datasets and evaluation procedures. The DARPA-sponsored Cyber Panel Correlation Technology Validation (CTV) effort, carried out in 2002 [Haines et al., 2003], was motivated by the need to assess correlation systems. This evaluation was performed on a testbed network with 59 hosts that were divided into four protected enclaves and one part that represented the public Internet. Several runs of 14 different attacks, divided into four classes (denial of service, data theft, web defacement, and backdoor installation), were performed, using only publicly available attack tools, while background traffic (e.g., web and mail traffic) was simulated using scripted applications. The alerts produced by a number of sensors during these attacks were collected and fed into the correlation tools being evaluated.

The truth files used in the Cyberpanel evaluation effort contain a basic description of the attacks. All attacks in the test were carried out in several steps. These steps did not overlapping and thus, the truth file sequentially lists all alerts produced by each attack.

To rank the different systems participating in the CTV effort, a suitable metrics for scoring each correlation system was developed. Although the group that organized the tests admits that this metrics was fairly "forgiving" (i.e., an artificially high score was awarded to all systems) [Haines et al., 2003], it currently represent the only existing metrics for evaluating correlation systems. According to this metrics, a correlation system should be penalized if too many alerts are generated (as an important task of alert correlation is to reduce the number of alerts that an administrator has to analyze).

The notion of "too many alerts" is defined using *result sets (RS)*. In [Haines et al., 2003], a result set is defined as: "Each correlator outputs an ordered list of reports (alerts). Given a designated *correlation threshold* (CT), RS is the set of reports with the highest priority, whose size is at most CT% of the underlying sensor alert set." This means that the result set contains a certain fraction of the alerts with the highest priority. The fraction is determined by the correlation threshold, which is set to a value such that the result set is of a size that is manageable for a system administrator.

Based on the result sets, two classes of metrics are used in the CTV scoring system: the *detection metrics* and the *target metrics*. The detection metrics (DM) measures how effective the correlator is at detecting attacks. The target metrics (TM) measures how effective the correlator is at detecting attacks *and* also reporting the corresponding target of the attack. Both metrics classes consists of 3 different metrics:

- DM1: An attack step is detected by at least on alert in RS.

- DM2: Two or more attack steps are combined into a single alert in RS.

- DM3: An attack step is detected and reported as a single alert in RS and the detection is based on alerts from at least two different sensors.

The target metrics are similar to the detection metrics, but in addition it is required that the target IP is available in the correlated alert.

- TM1: DM1 is true and target IP is available.

- TM2: DM2 is true and target IP is available.

- TM3: DM3 is true and target IP is available.

The values for the different metrics is calculated by counting how many times the metrics constraint is satisfied. For instance if a correlator detects 7 attack steps, the DM1 value for the sensor is 7. Similarly if a correlator outputs an alert linking two different steps of an attack, its DM2 value increases by one. A more detailed description of the metrics used, and the result of the evaluation can be found in [Haines et al., 2003].

Defcon Capture the Flag Datasets

Another dataset that is commonly used for IDS evaluation is the Defcon 9 Capture The Flag (CTF) dataset. Defcon is a yearly underground hacking convention that includes a hacker competition called Capture The Flag. In this competition, each of a number of teams is given one host that has to be defended. Simultaneously, each competing team also attempts to break into the other teams' hosts. Upon successful compromise of another host, the attacking team is awarded points. During Defcon 9, all traffic on the competition network was recorded and made publicly available. The Defcon 9 dataset has several properties that makes it very different from "real world" network traffic. For instance it contains an artificial high amount of attack traffic, no background traffic, and only includes a small number of IP addresses. In spite of these shortcomings, this dataset is very useful for IDS testing as it represents a worst-case scenario of the amount of attack traffic an IDS will receive and thus can be used for stress testing.

2.2   Problems

The aforementioned datasets are a tremendous asset for the intrusion detection community, but they have problems that often make them unsuitable for the evaluation of the effectiveness of some of the components of the correlation process. First of all, some of the datasets were created to evaluate intrusion detection sensors and not to assess correlation tools. Therefore, the data collected does not include IDS alerts, which have to be generated by running specific sensors on the collected event streams. As a result, the alert stream associated with a dataset may be different if different sensors are utilized or if the configuration of the sensor is not the same. This, in turn, makes it harder to compare the results of correlation systems.

Another problem is that the offline nature of these datasets makes it impossible to perform real-time alert verification, where the victim of an attack is analyzed to determine if the attack is relevant or not. In addition, the impact of attacks on the protected network and on the mission that the network infrastructure supports are impossible to evaluate, due to the lack of a mission model and its relationship with the network assets. Finally, network health monitoring information is usually not provided, which makes it difficult to determine the actual impact of the attacks.

Also, the datasets presented all suffer from the fact that they are not representative of real world traffic. The Lincoln Lab datasets are all synthetically generated and questions have been raised about the realism of the background traffic models used [McHugh, 2000]. Also, none of the datasets presented was recorded on a network connected to the Internet. This could be a problem since Internet traffic usually contains a fairly large amount of anomalous traffic that is not created by any malicious behavior [Bellovin, 1992]. Datasets recorded in a network isolated from the Internet might not include these types of anomalies.

2.3 Correlation Evaluation Truth Files

The truth file used in a correlator evaluation should be the high-level plan behind the attacks contained in the test data. The plan should describe how each low-level alert is related to other alerts in the test data. For instance if two alerts are duplicates as a result of two network sensors seeing the same packet, the alerts in question should be marked as such. Also, on a higher abstraction level, attacks belonging to the same attack session should be grouped and any temporal dependencies between the alerts within the group should be expressed. For instance if the attack involves a scan followed by a break in, the truth file should include this fact.

The problem is that representing this information is difficult. There is no good definition of what is meant by a high-level plan, and, in addition, there is also no standardized way to express such a plan.

Another problem is that it is difficult to compare the output of a correlator to the plan contained in the truth file. Two widely different high-level views of an attack might both be correct. For example, consider a correlator that can perform two operations: Identify similar attacks across multiple hosts and identify a scan followed by a break in attempt. If this correlator encounters a series of scan-breakin attempts against multiple hosts, it may correlate this in different ways (see Figure 8.1 for two possibilities). The correlator can either

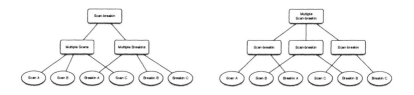

Figure 8.1. Two Possible Ways of Correlating the Same Data

choose to view this as a series of scans followed by a series of break in attempts, or as a series of scan-breakin attempts against multiple hosts. One might argue that in this case both views convey the same information to the operator of the system, but there is currently no good way of automatically determining this.

2.4   Factors Affecting the Alert Reduction Rate

Experiments have shown that the achieved alert reduction rate is highly dependent on the features of the dataset being processed. Also, a particular dataset that experiences a high reduction rate during one of the correlation steps might achieve poor reduction rates during other steps. It is therefore important to calculate reduction rates for different datasets when testing correlation systems. Also, it is useful to calculate the reduction rate during each step in addition to the total reduction rate.

Several properties of the datasets play a role in determining how much reduction is achieved at each step. These properties can roughly be divided into three different groups.

The first group is the topology of the defended network. For instance, if the defended network is very small (one or two hosts), it impossible to detect any large-scale IP sweeps. The network topology also includes the type of intrusion detection sensors that are deployed, as well as their configuration and placement. For instance, if two network sensors were placed such that most network traffic is observed by both sensors, the fusion rate would be higher compared to sensors placed such that most traffic is only observed by a single sensor.

The second group of properties is the characteristics of the attacks. For instance, a brute force password guessing attack could cause a very high reduction rate in the thread reconstruction step. Another example is the MIT Lincoln Lab 1999 data. This dataset does not contain any multistep attacks as the dataset was comprised of individual attacks only. Thus, no high-level attack patterns can be identified.

Finally, the metadata available for the correlation system plays an important role in how well the correlation is performed. The session reconstruction step needs information about which processes are listening to which port. Without this information, session reconstruction cannot be performed reliably. The alert verification step is also dependent on metadata. In particular, this component requires up-to-date information about which hosts are running services with known vulnerabilities.

Chapter 9

OPEN ISSUES

Although the fields of intrusion detection and alert correlation have evolved rapidly in the last years, there are still a number of problems that have not been solved satisfactorily. In addition, technological advances such as increasing network speeds or the increasing use of encrypted network traffic pose new challenges that have to be addressed. This chapter discusses open issues [Kemmerer and Vigna, 2002] in the field and sketches potential ways to tackle them. We first discuss intrusion detection in general and then concentrate on alert correlation in particular.

1. Intrusion Detection

For accurate intrusion detection, one requires reliable and complete data about the target system's activities. Reliable data collection is a complex issue in itself. Collecting information is expensive, and collecting the right information is important. Therefore, determining what information to log and where to collect it is a difficult problem.

Most operating systems offer some form of auditing, which provides a log of the operations performed by users and applications. These logs might be limited to the security-relevant events (such as failed login attempts) or they might offer a complete report on every system call invoked by every process. Similarly, routers and firewalls provide event logs for network activity. These logs might contain simple information, such as network connection openings and closings, or a complete record of every packet that appeared on the wire.

In general, the amount of system activity information a system collects is a tradeoff between overhead and effectiveness. A system that records every action in detail could have substantially degraded performance and, in addition, requires enormous disk storage. This is especially true when recording network traffic on high-speed networks. For example, collecting a complete log of network packets on a 100-Mbit Ethernet link could require hundreds of GBytes per day.

Therefore, it is important to decide which information is relevant with regard to the threat model and the security policy that is in place. For example, having your house alarm system monitor the water for pollution is an expensive activity that doesn't help detect burglars. On the other hand, if the house's threat model includes terrorist attacks, monitoring the pollution level might be reasonable.

Often, it is not possible to monitor all events that are potentially security relevant. For example, it is considered easy to monitor network traffic by setting up a machine with a network card in promiscuous mode and connect it to the interesting networks. However, the network could be deployed using a star topology with a switch in the center that forwards traffic only on the appropriate links. To solve this problem, the span port on the switch can be used. This span port is built to mirror all network traffic that is sent over the switch's backplane, potentially duplicating all packets that are forwarded. The problem is that the bandwidth of the backplane far exceeds the bandwidth of the span port, causing some packets to be dropped at the span port when the load is too high.

A simple scenario such as a switched Ethernet can already present a problematic environment for capturing a complete trace of network packets. The problem gets worse when considering high-speed networks. Gigabit Ethernet is common, and fast optical links are gaining popularity. The network nodes are also getting faster, processing more data and generating more audit logs. There are two possible ways to analyze the huge amount of data in real time: split the event stream or use peripheral network sensors.

In the first approach, a slicer component splits the event stream into slimmer, more manageable streams that the intrusion detection sensors can analyze in real time [Kruegel et al., 2002]. To do this, the whole event stream must be accessible at a single location. Therefore, researchers typically advocate stream splitting for centralized systems or network gateways.

A second approach is to deploy multiple sensors at the network periphery, close to the hosts that the system must protect. This approach assumes that by moving the analysis to the network's periphery, a natural partitioning of traffic will occur. The problem with this approach is that it is difficult to deploy and manage a highly distributed set of sensors. First of all, the correct sensor positioning can be difficult to determine. Attacks that depend on the network topology, such as routing- and spoofing-based attacks, require that detection sensors be placed at specific locations in the network. Second, there is a control and coordination issue. Networks are dynamic entities that evolve through time, and the threats evolve, too. New attacks are invented every day, and, therefore, the sensing infrastructure must evolve accordingly.

Encrypted network streams, such as SSL-protected HTTP connections and secure shell sessions, are another problem for network-based sensors. When a network-based sensor analyzes encrypted traffic, the analysis is limited to the packet headers. This significantly limits the classes of attacks that an IDS can identify. Based on packet headers, it is often only possible to detect attacks that can be characterized by the amount of traffic or the source and destination of packets. This includes denial of service or scan attempts, but leaves out important attacks such as buffer overflows. Even when an infrastructure exists that provides the IDS with the keys necessary to decrypt the network traffic, the cryptographic operations provide a significant computational overhead that needs to be handled. The problem of encrypted traffic is made worse by the increasing popularity of VPNs (virtual private networks) and IPSec [IPSec, 2004] that transparently encrypt all network traffic.

However, problems are not restricted to network-based sensors. When collecting data on closed-source operating systems such as Windows, it is not possible to extend the auditing subsystem to include information that might be required. Even when the operating system source is available (e.g., Linux), users usually need to upgrade the OS kernel to obtain the improved auditing functionality. This presents a barrier that often prevents host-based intrusion detection sensors from leaving the research labs and achieve widespread deployment.

Another problem is the limited auditing support in many applications. One reason is that application auditing, or logging, is done primarily for the purposes of debugging and accounting, and not for security. As a result, logging is often done after a transaction completes (successfully or not). However, logging at the end of an transaction might be too late because a successful attack can redirect the flow of execution before this point and thus evade logging. To solve this problem, it is often necessary to insert additional audit routines to get access to the application data *before* it is processed. Sometimes, getting the appropriate audit data is a problem by itself. Consider the situation of a Java Virtual Machine (JVM). In the case of a JVM, many Java threads are concurrently executing within a single virtual machine environment. In this environment, all Java threads are mapped onto a single operating system process. The granularity of the data, provided by a OS-based audit facility, is not sufficient to analyze the behavior of particular threads within the JVM. In addition, the malicious actions of a single Java application may trigger a response that disables an entire execution environment. To overcome these limitations, a thread-level auditing facility for the Java Virtual Machine is required.

Besides data gathering, data processing is still not satisfying. The challenge is to develop a system that is able to detect all the attacks and produce a minimal number of false positives. Misuse-based systems produce few false positives but do not detect unknown attacks. Anomaly-based systems are able to detect new attacks but typically produce many false positives. There are some projects that try to combine the advantages of the two approaches, by using a hybrid approach. An example is Emerald [Neumann and Porras, 1999], which adopts both a statistical anomaly detection unit and a signature-based inference unit, but the success has been limited so far.

A major problem with anomaly detection research is its focus on data modeling. It is assumed that it is easy to get input data that reflects the differences between attacks and normal behavior and the only real problem is to find the right techniques to distinguish between these classes. As a result, many approaches are evaluated on datasets (e.g., KDDCup '99 [KDDCup, 1999]) that represent real attacks very poorly. As a result, many systems are just trained on artifacts of the test data and fail to deliver consistent results on real audit data.

A third open issue besides data gathering and data processing is response. An intrusion detection system's response is its output or action upon detecting a problem. This response can take many different forms; the most common is to generate an alert that describes the detected intrusion. There are also more aggressive responses, such as paging a system administrator, sounding a siren, or even mounting a counter attack.

A counter attack might include reconfiguring a router to block the attacker's IP address or even attacking the culprit. Obviously, aggressive responses can be dangerous, since they could be launched against innocent victims. For example, a hacker may attack a network using spoofed traffic (i.e., traffic that appears to come from a certain address, but that is actually generated elsewhere). If the intrusion detection system detects the attack and reconfigures the network routers to block traffic from that address, it effectively executes a denial of service attack against the impersonated site. One possibility to solve the problem of self-inflicting denial of service is to compare the expected impact of a response to the expected impact of a successful attack and choose the lesser evil.

2. Alert Correlation

One problem that is also true for intrusion detection systems in general but that is particularly severe for correlation systems is evaluation. When someone develops and implements a new correlation approach, experimental evidence has to be provided to show that the system works as intended. The evaluation of a system is required to compare a system to the current state-of-the-art and to provide direction for further research efforts. However, it is difficult to develop an objective intrusion detection "benchmark". One problem is the fact that once the attacks in a benchmark are published, it is easy to tune an IDS to detect all of them (possible with no false positives). Another problem is that it requires considerable effort to create benchmarks. As a result, only a few IDS benchmarks were created (as described in the previous chapter), with their own set of problems. The situation is worse when creating benchmarks to evaluate alert correlation systems. One one hand, data from different locations and sensors is required. Therefore, it is necessary to set up multiple sensors that deliver different aspects of an attack scenario. On the other hand, it is easier to develop individual attacks than complete attack scenarios, which typically consist of multiple stages.

An area that is currently the focus of research interest is *intent recognition*. The idea of intent recognition is to deduce strategies and objectives of attackers, based on attack scenarios that are output by the alert correlation system. Intent recognition is related to impact analysis as both approaches attempt to draw conclusions from the available alert data. In addition, both approaches require a model of the network and the assets. The difference is that the focus of intent recognition is on the intruder and her possible next steps. The idea is to predict likely actions that an intruder might perform in the future to reach a particular goal. Impact analysis, on the other hand, is more concerned with the effects of already existing threats to the proper operation of vital network services.

Several other open issues related to alert correlation have been discussed in their respective chapters. Important examples are the lack of a common semantics for intrusion detection alerts (as discussed in Chapter 4), the large number of false positives that complicate analysis of later correlation stages (as discussed in Chapter 5), and the problem of sanitization of audit data to allow sharing (as discussed in Chapter 6).

Chapter 10

CONCLUSIONS

In this book, we introduced the reader to intrusion detection and alert correlation, two important weapons in the arsenal of a security officer. These tools are complementary to more traditional network security mechanisms, such as firewalls and cryptography, which attempt to prevent security policy violations. By supporting early warning and focused response, intrusion detection and alert correlation systems provide another layer of defense when the first security perimeter is penetrated.

The first part of the book provided an overview of intrusion detection and its role with regard to other network security mechanisms. We described different approaches to collect and analyze event data to find evidence of malicious activity. Unfortunately, individual intrusion detection systems can cover only parts of the event space and parts of the attack space. That is, a single IDS can process only a limited number of different types of input data, and it can identify only a limited number of attacks. This naturally leads to the integration of the output of different intrusion detection systems into a unified stream. This stream is then analyzed to identify attacks whose evidence may be collected by different sensors or whose components may be scattered in time and space. This analysis process is commonly called *alert correlation*.

The second part of the book described the different steps of the alert correlation process and introduced a general *correlation pipeline*. The components of the correlation pipeline deal with alerts at different levels of granularity, exploiting different temporal and spatial relationships. In the initial steps, alerts are collected and properly prepared for further processing. Then, alerts that are closely related in space and time are fused and combined. Finally, high-level structures are identified. These high-level alerts correlate attacks occurring at different locations in the network that represent complex intrusion scenarios.

In the third part of this book, we presented a novel correlation algorithm that significantly differs from traditional correlation approaches in that no centralized components are involved. We described the challenges that need to be solved and the limitations that need to be imposed to realize a system that detects intrusions in a completely peer-to-peer fashion.

Finally, in the last part of the book, the problems of evaluating intrusion detection systems and, in particular, correlation systems were discussed. We presented well-known efforts to provide realistic test data and the problems that are related to these benchmarks. In addition, a chapter was dedicated to the discussion of open research problems and directions towards which research could move over the next few years. This underlines the fact that although intrusion detection and alert correlation are effective techniques to identify intruders in large networks, not all problems are solved. Constant effort is necessary to deal with existing and emerging issues and shortcomings. For example, it is necessary to address the problem of detection evasion. As attackers increasingly expect intrusion detection systems to be installed at the victims' sites, they invest more effort in creating sophisticated, stealthy attacks that are not identified by the existing intrusion detection infrastructure.

We hope that we were able to provide a comprehensive overview of the functioning of intrusion detection and alert correlation, as well as the different techniques that are currently used. However, we also want to convey the message that intrusion detection is not a "solved problem." Instead, it is an enthralling area of active research with immediate practical implications. While attackers are constantly looking for means to break the security of computer systems, it is the task of the defender to come up with novel solutions to thwart these attempts.

References

AES (2001). Advanced Encryption Standard. National Institute of Standards and Technology, US Department of Commerce, FIPS 197.

Allen, J., Christie, A., Fithen, W., McHugh, J., Pickel, J., and Stoner, E. (2000). State of the Practice of Intrusion Detection Technologies. Technical Report CMU/SEI-99TR-028, Carnagie Mellon, Software Engineering Institute.

Almgren, M. and Lindqvist, U. (2001). Application-Integrated Data Collection for Security Monitoring. In Lee, W., Mé, L., and Wespi, A., editors, *Recent Advances in Intrusion Detection (RAID)*, Lecture Notes in Computer Science, pages 22–36. Springer.

Asaka, M., Taguchi, A., and Goto, S. (1999). The Implementation of IDA: An Intrusion Detection Agent System. In *11th FIRST Conference on Computer Security Incident Handling and Response*.

Axelsson, S. (1999). The Base-Rate Fallacy and Its Implications for the Difficulty of Intrusion Detection. In *ACM Conference on Computer and Communications Security*, pages 1–7.

Bace, R. and Mell, P. (2001). Intrusion Detection Systems. Technical Report NIST SP 800-31, National Institute of Standards and Technology.

Balasubramaniyan, J. S., Garcia-Fernandez, J. O., Isacoff, D., Spafford, E., and Zamboni, D. (1998). An Architecture for Intrusion Detection using Autonomous Agents. In *14th Annual Computer Security Applications Conference (ACSAC)*.

Balepin, I., Maltsev, S., Rowe, J., and Levitt, K. (2004). Using Specification-Based Intrusion Detection for Automated Response. In *Recent Advances in Intrusion Detection (RAID)*.

Bellovin, S. M. (1993). Packets Found on an Internet. *Computer Communications Review*, 23(3):26–31.

Bellovin, S. M. (2001). Computer Security - An End State? *Communications of the ACM*, 44(3):131–132.

Bellovin, Steven M. (1992). Packets found on an internet. Technical report, AT&T Bell Laboratories.

Bugtraq (2004). Security mailing list. http://www.securityfocus.com.

Carzaniga, A., Rosenblum, D., and Wolf, A. (2000). Achieving scalability and expressiveness in an internet-scale event notification service. In *ACM Symposium on Principles of Distributed Computing*, pages 219–227, Portland OR, USA.

CERT (2003). CERT Statistics 2003. http://www.cert.org/stats/cert_stats.html.

Cheswick, W. and Bellovin, S. (1994). *Firewalls and Internet Security*. Addison-Wesley, Reading, Massachusetts, USA.

Cohen, F. (1999). Simulating Cyber Attacks, Defenses, and Consequences. `http://all.net/journal/ntb/simulate/simulate.html`.

Coulouris, G., Dollimore, J., and Kindberg, T. (1996). *Distributed Systems - Concepts and Design*. Addison-Wesley, Harlow, England, 2nd edition.

Crosbie, M. and Spafford, E. (1995). Defending a Computer System using Autonomous Agents. In *18th National Information Systems Security Conference*.

Cuppens, F. and Miege, A. (2002). Alert Correlation in a Cooperative Intrusion Detection Framework. In *IEEE Symposium on Security and Privacy*, Oakland, CA.

Curry, D. and Debar, H. (2003). Intrusion Detection Message Exchange Format: Extensible Markup Language (XML) Document Type Definition. `draft-ietf-idwg-idmef-xml-10.txt`.

CVE (2004). Common Vulnerabilities and Exposures. `http://www.cve.mitre.org/`.

Dacier, M., Debar, H., and Wespi, A. (1999). Towards a taxonomy of intrusion-detection systems. *Computer Networks*, 31(8):805–822.

de Queiroz, J. D., da Costa Carmo, L. F. R., and Pirmez, L. (1999). Micael: An Autonomous Mobile Agent System to Protect New Generation Networked Applications. In *2nd Annual Workshop on Recent Advances in Intrusion Detection*.

DES (1977). Data Encryption Standard. National Bureau of Standards, US Department of Commerce, FIPS 46-3.

Diffie, W. and Hellman, M. (1976). New Directions in Cryptography. *IEEE Transactions on Information Theory*, IT-22(6):644–654.

Eckmann, S.T., Vigna, G., and Kemmerer, R.A. (2002). STATL: An Attack Language for State-based Intrusion Detection. *Journal of Computer Security*, 10(1/2):71–104.

Flegel, U. (2002). Pseudonymizing Unix Log Files. In *Infrastructure Security Conference (InfraSec)*.

Floyd, S. and Paxson, V. (2001). Difficulties in Simulating the Internet. *IEEE/ACM Transactions on Networking*, 9(4):392–403.

Ghosh, A. K., Wanken, J., and Charron, F. (1998). Detecting Anomalous and Unknown Intrusions Against Programs. In Akers, D., editor, *Annual Computer Security Applications Conference (ACSAC)*, pages 259–267. IEEE Computer Society.

Haines, J., Ryder, D.K., Tinnel, L., and Taylor, S. (2003). Validation of Sensor Alert Correlators. *IEEE Security & Privacy Magazine*, 1(1):46–56.

Handley, M., Paxson, V., and Kreibich, C. (2001). Network Intrusion Detection: Evasion, Traffic Normalization, and End-to-End Protocol Semantics. In *10th USENIX Security Symposium*.

Helman, P. and Liepins, G. (1993). Statistical Foundations of Audit Trail Analysis for the Detection of Computer Misuse. *IEEE Transactions on Software Engineering*, 19(9):886–901.

Hofmeyr, S. A., Forrest, S., and Somayaji, A. (1998). Intrusion Detection Using Sequences of System Calls. *Journal of Computer Security*, 6(3):151–180.

Ilgun, K., Kemmerer, R. A., and Porras, P. A. (1995). State Transition Analysis: A Rule-Based Intrusion Detection System. *IEEE Transactions on Software Engineering*, 21(3).

IPSec (2004). IP Sec. Protocol. `http://www.ietf.org/html.charters/ipsec-charter.html`.

Kahn, C., Porras, P. A., Staniford-Chen, S., and Tung, B. (1998). A Common Intrusion Detection Framework. `http://gost.isi.edu/cidf/papers/cidf-jcs.ps`.

KDDCup (1999). The Third International Knowledge Discovery and Data Mining Tools Competition. `http://kdd.ics.uci.edu/databases/kddcup99/kddcup99.html`.

Kemmerer, R. A. and Vigna, G. (2002). Intrusion Detection: A Brief History and Overview. *IEEE Computer*, 35(4):27–30.

Ko, C., Ruschitzka, M., and Levitt, K. (1997). Execution Monitoring of Security-Critical Programs in Distributed Systems: A Specification-based Approach. In *IEEE Symposium on Security and Privacy*, pages 175–187.

Kruegel, C. and Toth, T. (2001). An efficient, IP based Solution to the 'Logical Timestamp Wrapping' Problem. In *6th International Conference on Telecommunication*.

Kruegel, C., Toth, T., and Kirda, E. (2001). Sparta - A Security Policy Reinforcement Tool for Large Networks. In *IFIP Conference on Advances in Network and Distributed Systems Security*. Kluwer Academic Publishers.

Kruegel, C., Valeur, F., Vigna, G., and Kemmerer, R. A. (2002). Stateful Intrusion Detection for High-Speed Networks. In *IEEE Symposium on Security and Privacy*, pages 285–294.

Kumar, S. and Spafford, E. H. (1994). A Pattern Matching Model for Misuse Intrusion Detection. In *Proceedings of the 17th National Computer Security Conference*, pages 11–21.

Lamport, L. (1978). Time, Clocks and the Ordering of Events in a Distributed System. *Communications of the ACM*, 21(7):558–65.

Landwehr, C. E., Bull, A. R., McDermott, J. P., and Choi, W. S. (1994). A Taxonomy of Computer Program Security Flaws. *ACM Computing Surveys (CSUR)*, 26(3):211–254.

LIDS (2004). Linux Intrusion Detection System. http://www.lids.org/.

Lindqvist, U. and Porras, P. A. (1999). Detecting Computer and Network Misuse Through the Production-Based Expert System Toolset (P-BEST). In *IEEE Symposium on Security and Privacy*, pages 146–161, Oakland, California. IEEE Computer Society Press, Los Alamitos, California.

Lonvick, C. (2001). The BSD syslog Protocol. RFC 3164.

Loscocco, P. and Smalley, S. (2001). Integrating Flexible Support for Security Policies into the Linux Operating System. In *Freenix Track of Usenix Annual Technical Conference*.

Lunt, T. F. (1993). Detecting Intruders in Computer Systems. In *5th Canadian Conference on Auditing and Computer Technology*.

Malan, G. R., Watson, D., Jahanian, F., and Howell, P. (2000). Transport and Application Protocol Scrubbing. In *INFOCOM (3)*, pages 1381–1390.

McHugh, J. (2000). Testing Intrusion Detection Systems: A Critique of the 1998 and 1999 DARPA Intrusion Detection System Evaluations as Performed by Lincoln Laboratory. *ACM Transactions on Information and System Security (TISSEC)*, 3(4):262–294.

MIT Lincoln Laboratory (2000). DARPA Intrusion Detection Evaluation. http://www.ll.mit.edu/IST/ideval/.

Moore, D., Paxson, V., Savage, S., Shannon, C., Staniford, S., and Weaver, N. (2003). The Spread of the Sapphire/Slammmer Worm. http://www.cs.berkeley.edu/~nweaver/sapphire/.

Morin, B., Me, L., Debar, H., and Ducasse, M. (2002). M2D2: A Formal Data Model for IDS Alert Correlation. In *Recent Advances in Intrusion Detection (RAID)*, pages 115–137, Zurich, Switzerland.

Mutz, D., Vigna, G., and Kemmerer, R. A. (2003). An Experience Developing an IDS Stimulator for the Black-Box Testing of Network Intrusion Detection Systems. In *Annual Computer Security Applications Conference (ACSAC)*, Las Vegas, Nevada.

Neumann, P. G. and Porras, P. A. (1999). Experience with EMERALD to Date. In *First USENIX Workshop on Intrusion Detection and Network Monitoring*, pages 73–80, Santa Clara, California.

Ning, P., Cui, Y., and Reeves, D. S. (2002). Constructing Attack Scenarios through Correlation of Intrusion Alerts. In *ACM Conference on Computer and Communications Security (CCS)*, pages 245–254, Washington, D.C.

Ning, P. and Xu, D. (2003). Learning Attack Strategies from Intrusion Alert. In *ACM Conference on Computer and Communications Security (CCS)*, Washington, DC.

Northcutt, S. (1999). *Network Intrusion Detection - An Analyst's handbook.* New Riders, Indianapolis, USA.

Pang, R. and Paxson, V. (2003). A High-level Programming Environment for Packet Trace Anonymization and Transformation. In *ACM SIGCOMM.*

Patton, S., Yurcik, W., and Doss, D. (2001). An Achilles Heel in Signature-Based IDS: Squealing False Positives in SNORT. http://www.raid-symposium.org/raid2001/program.html.

Porras, P., Schnackenberg, D., Staniford-Chen, S., Stillman, M., and Wu, F. (1998). The Common Intrusion Detection Framework Architecture. http://www.isi.edu/gost/cidf/drafts/architecture.txt.

Porras, P.A. and Neumann, P.G. (1997). EMERALD: Event Monitoring Enabling Responses to Anomalous Live Disturbances. In *National Information Systems Security Conference.*

Postel, J. (1981). Internet Protocol. RFC 791.

Ptacek, T. H. and Newsham, T. N. (1998). Insertion, Evasion, and Denial of Service: Eluding Network Intrusion Detection. Technical report, Secure Networks, Inc.

Ranum, M. (2000). Intrusion Detection and Network Forensics. In *M1 Tutorial - USENIX Security 2000,* Denver, Colorado, USA.

Rescorla, E. (2003). Security holes... Who cares? In Paxson, V., editor, *USENIX Security Symposium,* pages 75–90. USENIX.

Rivest, R. L., Shamir, A., and Adleman, L. A. (1978). A Method for obtaining Digital Signatures and Public-Key Cryptosystems. *Communications of the ACM,* 21(2):120–126.

Roesch, M. (1999). Snort - Lightweight Intrusion Detection for Networks. In Parter, D., editor, *Large Installation System Administraton (LISA),* pages 229–238. USENIX.

Schneier, Bruce (1996). *Applied Cryptography.* John Wiley & Sons, Inc., New York, USA, 2nd edition.

Shankar, U. and Paxson, V. (2003). Active Mapping: Resisting NIDS Evasion Without Altering Traffic. In *IEEE Symposium on Security and Privacy.*

Snapp, S., Brentano, J., Dias, G. V., Goan, T. L., Heberlein, L. T., Ho, C., Levitt, K. N., Mukherjee, B., Smaha, S. E., Grance, T., Teal, D. M., and Mansur, D. (1991). DIDS (Distributed Intrusion Detection System) - Motivation, Architecture and an early Prototype. In *14th National Security Conference,* pages 167–176.

Snot (2004). A packet generator. http://www.stolenshoes.net/sniph/.

Stallings, William (2000). *Network Security Essentials - Applications and Standards.* Prentice Hall, Englewood Cliffs, New Jersey, USA.

Staniford, S., Cheung, S., Crawford, R., Dilger, M., Frank, J., Hoagland, J., Levitt, K., Wee, C., Yip, R., and Zerkle, D. (1996). GrIDS - A Graph Based Intrusion Detection System For Large Networks. In *20th National Information Systems Security Conference,* volume 1, pages 361–370.

Staniford, S., Hoagland, J. A., and McAlerney, J. M. (2000). Practical Automated Detection of Stealthy Portscans. In *ACM Computer and Communications Security IDS Workshop.*

Stick (2004). IDS stress tool. http://www.eurocompton.net/stick/projects8.html.

Sun Microsystems, Inc. (1991). *Installing, Administering, and Using the Basic Security Module.* 2550 Garcia Ave., Mountain View, CA 94043.

Tan, K. M. C., Killourhy, K. S., and Maxion, R. A. (2002). Undermining an Anomaly-Based Intrusion Detection System Using Common Exploits. In Wespi, A., Vigna, G., and Deri, L., editors, *Recent Advances in Intrusion Detection (RAID),* Lecture Notes in Computer Science, pages 54–73. Springer.

Tan, K. M. C. and Maxion, R. A. (2002). Why 6? Defining the Operational Limits of Stide, an Anomaly-Based Intrusion Detector. In *IEEE Symposium on Security and Privacy,* pages 188–201.

Tanenbaum, Andrew S. and van Steen, Maarten (2002). *Distributed Systems - Principles and Paradigms*. Prentice Hall, Englewood Cliffs, New Jersey, USA.

tcpdump (2002). Tcpdump and Libpcap Documentation. http://www.tcpdump.org/.

Toth, T. and Kruegel, C. (2002). Evaluating the Impact of Automated Intrusion Response Mechanisms. In *18th Annual Computer Security Applications Conference (ACSAC)*. IEEE Computer Society Press.

Undercoffer, J., Joshi, A., and Pinkston, J. (2003). Modeling Computer Attacks: An Ontology for Intrusion Detection. In *6th International Symposium on Recent Advances in Intrusion Detection*.

U.S. Department of Defense (1985). Department of Defense Trusted Computer System Evaluation Criteria.

Wagner, D. and Soto, P. (2002). Mimicry Attacks on Host-Based Intrusion Detection Systems. In *ACM Conference on Computer and Communications Security (CCS)*.

White, Gregory B., Fisch, Eric A., and Pooch, Udo W. (1996). Cooperating Security Managers: A peer-based intrusion detection system. *IEEE Network*, pages 20–23.

x509 (2002). Public-Key Infrastructure X.509. The Internet Engineering Task Force.

Xu, J., Fan, J., Ammar, M., and Moon, S. (2002). On the design and performance of prefix preserving IP trace traffic anonymization. In *ACM SIGCOMM Internet Measurement Workshop*.

Index